SHOC

Virginia Boston

With introductions
by Danny Baker &
Ian Rakoff

Photographs by
Derek Ridgers
Annette Wetherman
Walt Davidson
Ray Stevenson
Richard Braine
Sheila Rock
Mick Rock
Erica Echenberg
Dennis Morris
Jonh Ingham
Kevin Cummins
Bob Gruen
Peter Kodick
J.R.
Harry F. Murlowski
Norma Morrisey
Pete of Shews
Paulo
Jo-anne Atkinson
Jane Ashley
Jill Furmanovsky

Plexus, London

WAVE

First printing 1978

ISBN 085965 020 0

Designed by Derek Ridgers

Printed in Great Britain by
Dillcourt Limited, London N1.
Filmset in Helvetica

The author thanks the following for
kind permission to publish their lyrics
The Clash, *Remote Control*
©Strummer/Jones
The Jam, *Art School* ©Weller
Sham 69, *Rip-off* ©Pursey/Parsons
The Clash, *Complete Control*
©Strummer/Jones
The Clash, *Career Opportunities*
©Strummer/Jones
The Clash, *Garageland*
©Strummer/Jones
The Sex Pistols, *Anarchy in the UK*
©1976 Jones/Rotten/Matlock/Cook
The Sex Pistols, *God Save the Queen*
©1977 Jones/Rotten/Matlock/Cook
The Sex Pistols, *Pretty Vacant*
©1977 Jones/Rotten/Matlock/Cook
The Clash, *White Riot*
©Strummer/Jones
The Clash, *1977* ©Strummer/Jones
The Damned, *Neat, Neat, Neat*
©Stiff Records and Rock Music Co
The Stranglers, *Get a Grip on Yourself*
©1977 April Music Ltd/Albion Music Ltd
The Jam, *In the City*
©Lupus Music Co Ltd
The Jam, *All Around the World*
©Lupus Music Co Ltd
The Jam, *Time for Truth*
©Lupus Music Co Ltd
Chelsea, *Right to Work*
©Step Forward Music
Generation X, *Your Generation*
©Idol/James
Generation X, *Day by Day* ©Idol/James
Buzzcocks, *Breakdown*
©Virgin Music Publishing Ltd
Buzzcocks, *Boredom*
©Virgin Music Publishing Ltd
The Slits, *Number One Enemy*
©Palmolive/Arri Up
The Slits, *Love and Romance*
©Viv Albertine
The Adverts, *One Chord Wonder*
©Adverse Noise Music Publishing
The Adverts, *Bored Teenagers*
©Adverse Noise Music Publishing
Sham 69, *Oxford Street*
©Pursey/Parsons
X-Ray Specs, *Oh Bondage Up Yours!*
©Poly Styrene
Alternative TV, *How Much Longer*
©Mark P.

'It was going to go down as one of the most boring decades in history I should think musically . . . The seventies will now be a landmark in history, because of what's gone on and it's all to do with young people'. *Jordan, Punk Personality*

'When it all started off I was amazed, I've never seen any movement move so quick, right, tremendous potential. All the kids caught on to something, they got on to an idea. They had all this energy in 'em'. *Don Letts, Roxy disc jockey*

'In the 1950s and 1960s kids had a little more to do, more access to things. They overtook the music business, the music papers, you had new disc jockeys, pirate stations, swinging London. That's all gone . . . These kids had to find expression and rock'n'roll seemed an adequate means. They can't turn round and say The Who's Peter Townshend is great—he's old enough to be their father'. *Malcolm McLaren, Manager of Sex Pistols*

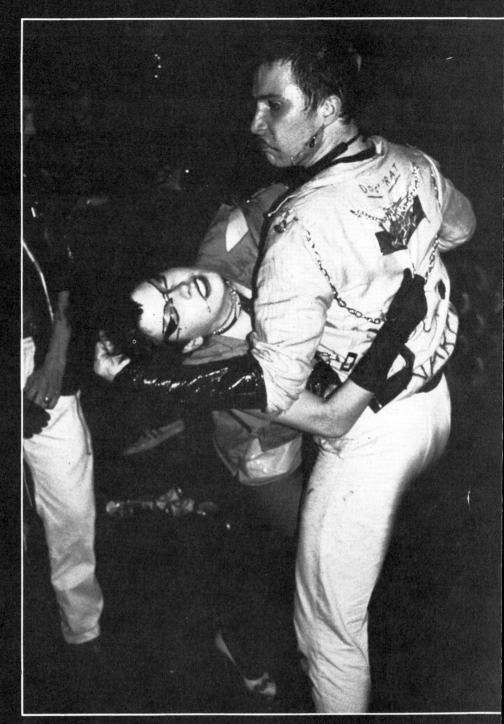

'Really, the generation of 16-18 year olds haven't had a music they could call their own. Woodstock's no good for them, nor boys and girls going out together under the silvery moon. Their reality's a lot bleaker than that. So it's back to three-minute songs, simple melodies, thumping it out. The content is a bit heavier because it's 1977 and not 1957'. *Malcolm McLaren, Manager of Sex Pistols*

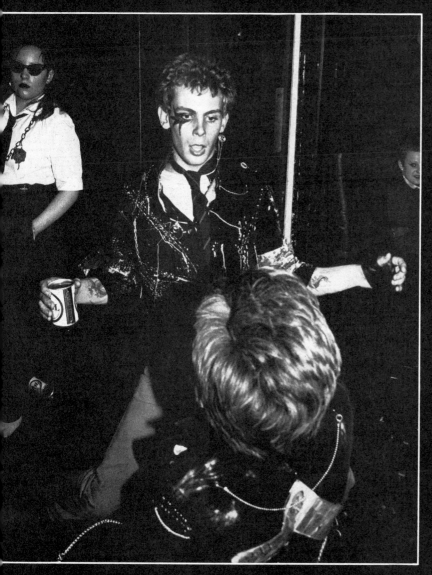

'Rock'n'roll is supposed to be fun. You remember fun don'tcha? You're supposed to enjoy it'. *Johnny Rotten*

SNIFFIN' GLUE...
AND OTHER ROCK'N'ROLL HABITS
FOR DEPTFORD YOBS! ⑩ JUNE-1977.

CHELSEA + JOHNNY MOPED
+ JOHN CALE, WHITE RIOT TOUR.

'All you kids out there who read *SG* don't be satisfied with what *we* write. Go out and start your own fanzines or send reviews to the established papers. Let's really get on their nerves, flood the market with punk-writing'
Mark P.

Sniffin' Glue
1st Issue—July 1976
Deptford, London
'No-one can define Punk Rock, it's all about rock in its lowest form—on the level of the streets. Kids jamming together in the Dad's garage, poor equipment, tight clothes, empty heads (nothing to do now you've left school) and model shops. Punk Rock's all those things'.
Mark P. (19)

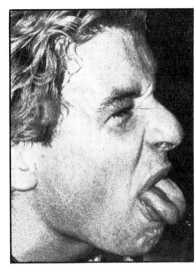

'Through the astral planes of
    Aslan
The runs detect the logic of
    my inner spans . . .'

'Hey LA you look real good
    today
Let me ease on down in your
    mellow sunshine . . .'

'Got me a hard lovin' rock'n'roll
    woman
Let me know I'm her hard
    boogie man.'
(See *Melody Maker* '67 to
date . . .)

Oh yeah?

'It's so grey in London Town,
Panda cars movin' around.
Here it comes
Eleven o'clock,
Where can we go now?'
(The Clash, *Remote Control*
© Strummer/Jones)

But what did I care, I was
from the East End and we're
the salt of the earth. My school
didn't bother about silly things
like education. USSR is in
Russia and they have
communism which is about
Chairman Mao. 'Next week a
councillor will be visiting
school so any boys without full
uniform will be caned. Should
he come into a lesson you will

stand and say "good morning,
sir". When he leaves you will
rise again and say "goodbye
and thank you, sir".' Working
class kids say 'sir' a lot. Six
years of copying from books
that millions of other kids are
copying from all over the
country in an obscene blanket
'learning' that drums any
character or ambition out of
you. At the end of that you are
given five minutes with a man
who fumbles for the bit of
paper to find out if you're the
maths or metalwork model,
and then recommends the
office or the site.
    And it's 'sir' for the next sixty
years.

'Who makes the rules that
    make people select?
Who is to judge that your ways
    are correct?
The media as watchdog is
    absolute shit,
The TV's telling you what to
    think.'
(The Jam, *Art School* ©Weller)

'All foreign feet down Oxford
    Street,
Faces from places I've never
    been,
All the shops and restaurants,
Asking for money I haven't got.
It's just a fake
Make no mistake
A rip-off for us
But a Rolls for them.'
(Sham 69, *Rip-off*
©Pursey/Parsons)

And still people wonder what
we see in Punk Rock.

'You're dirty. You're filthy.
You're never gonna last.'
(The Clash, *Complete Control*
©Strummer/Jones)

I was never aware that I was
thick, bored and being used
until I was allowed to think.
    So long as the pubs opened
at half past five, so long as I
could be seen to 'weigh in' at
the end of the night, so long as
the wages were good (hey
Dave, it's filthy work, shitty
hours and I can hardly stand
when I get home, but the
wages are good . . .) so long
as the telly was on and *The*

Sun had tits on page three.
    Sedation.

'They offered me the office,
    offered me the shop,
They said I'd better take any
    job they got,
Do you wanna make tea at the
    BBC,

Do you really wanna be a cop.
Career opportunities the ones
    that never knock.
Every job they offer is to keep
    you off the dock,
'Cos career opportunities the
    ones that never knock.'
(The Clash, *Career
Opportunities*
©Strummer/Jones)

    To anyone involved in punk
it is obscene that anyone of
your same age/background
could be dictated to and con-
trolled by the newspapers. It is
obscene that Zandra Rhodes
designs 'punk chic' clothes
that retail at three-figure prices
when in the same city people
work six days a week for £20.

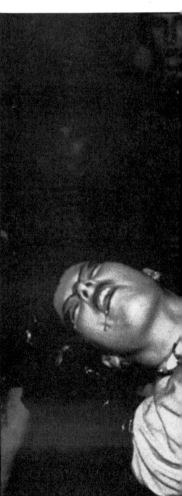

don't want to hear about
what the rich are doing.
They think they're so clever.
They think they're so right
The truth is only known by
guttersnipes.'
The Clash, *Garageland,*
(Strummer/Jones)

There are no 'sirs' in punk
rock (although some of the
latecoming fans tend to hold
the bigger bands in awe while
in the same breath putting
them down as 'stars'). When
the right band is playing, the
frustration of all the shit
around you is released, given
voice, and the strength of
knowing others feel the same
way has more passion than
any soap box, book or
pamphlet with well thought out
and structured argument
could touch on. That
suppressed voice, trodden
down through years of character training in the ignorance
factories, can shout FUCK
YOU at 'sir', the Queen, the

fuckin' Pope—anyone. WE
ARE THE PUNK ROCKERS.
And then up pops Mr
Average and says 'but you
don't even play in tune . . .'
Can you feel it?
All that anyone ever wants to
know about is the safety-pin
trip, 'cos obviously we are all
sick morons. The schmoosick
industry with all its tailored
suits, cocktails, product, well
planned 'crazes', boxed sets
and chain stores will never be
harmed. One 'in-pay' DJ and a
payola phone call could get
the nation's youth on any kick
it fancied—like the sickening
Glen Miller mania where kids
dressed like old men and were
shown that 'real music' could
only be made by the mature.
You too could make *The Sun*
centre pages in that £50 US
airman's outfit. For years the
orders came from above and
if you were really lucky your
application might be chosen
from the millions applying for a
£6 seat to see one of the

'legends' condescending to
their bi-annual one-off. Such
Treats. Freddie Mercury
toasting his audience, 'May
you all have Champagne for
breakfast . . .'
While the audience
screamed for more (why?)
there was Mick chatting to
Princess Margaret backstage
('I do wish they'd keep it down
. . .'). Middle classers. Rich
kids. Tickets on the door
because 'I know Elton' but
forget the names of his songs
because it's the party after that
counts ('I hear Rod may be
there'). Freddie, Elton, Mick,
Rodders. . . .
When you see tired old
businessmen with paunches,
running up drug bills that
make your monthly wage
seem like a cabbie's tip, you
feel sick. When you see 'rock
stars' hopping into planes with
double-barrelled, thick-headed
debs ten minutes after they
have told you to stop bother-
ing them for autographs, that
is sick. When you see blokes
the same as yourself on stage,
hard edged and real, putting
all this down in violent energy
as opposed to simpering,
foppish pantomime, that is
punk rock.
There is no bigger crime
than being cheated out of the
years that matter.
Working class kids are
usually brainwashed into
believing in a mythical one day
when it will be all right. A nice
cosy nuclear family, a nice
cosy old age. Mindless.
I've been told that one day I'll
see the error and waste of my
ways and then it will be too
late. Too late for what? A
government training course?
Two up, two down? I ain't
gonna be forty and regret,
because I know that I had
nobody to answer to, nobody
to satisfy, nobody to call 'sir'.
These are the years. We are
the Punk Rockers.
DANNY BAKER
Editor, *Sniffin' Glue*

Punk sprang to the forefront of new musical trends as a reaction to the patterns established by the 'swinging sixties'. Its quick birth and rapid growth owe much to the nature of British society in the seventies, as in the oldest parliamentary democracy in the industrial world, modern problems tend to appear first. Inflation and urban congestion blended with a potential 1984 setting offer little escape for the young, so Punk is an expression in a wasteland of despair. The music is a simple easy-to-feel-and-follow, raw, repeating beat played with stunning volume. There is a dance to go with it that doesn't have to be learned — anyone can pogo — bounce up and down. The songs cater for the fury of youth. They sing of the dole queue, no feelings, boredom and frustration. They laugh at the absurdity of values that no longer serve, only bind, chain, imprison and dehumanize.

The rapid growth of Punk has also been helped by the pub system. As their parents met in pubs so too did the kids — as soon as they reached drinking age. Pubs are places for live entertainment and new groups have often got started from them. The hours are brief, but then so is Punk music. Quick drinking, hard rough music and fast pogoing until closing time with the kids getting a chance to scream out, dance out and act out their rebelliousness. Unlike halls, clubs and theatres, which inhibit entry, pubs are situated at street level and project an easy accessibility.

The Sex Pistols were without question in the forefront of the new musical awakening. So much so that their story is worth telling in full later. After them came new groups with amazing rapidity. Years of practise and rehearsals became a thing of the past. Groups got together, rehearsing and experimenting while they were performing on stage. Like the immediacy of the music, life had to be carried forward quickly, because there wasn't time.

The distance between stage and audience has shrunk. Superstardom barriers are gone. Kids can leap on stage, swirling among the musicians as if they are part of the act. Everyone can be an artist for five seconds. The stage appearance, whether studied or indifferent, is as important as the music. The stance of the punk groups describes not only their style but their attitudes as well.

Some of the groups now rocketing to success started as innocent products of rebellion. Some are revamped older groups cashing in on a popular music fashion. Some are just ambitious youngsters with talent and skill, determined to make money. Each is motivated in a different way.

The Clash started with a name to clash against all and everything. Their stance has emerged as one of seething criticism and perceptive awareness, allying themselves with the cause of the bored, unemployed teenager. They deny that they are political, but just want to encourage people to think for themselves. Their history is similar to the Pistols'. A catalogue of outrage, cancellation, bannings and grovelling for venues. *Remote Control, London's Burning, Hate and War, White Riot* are song titles that typify their sentiment and attitude.

Whether political or not, the immediate relevance of their lyrics is marked with extraordinary lucidity. Audience participation has been extreme, with gigs ending in ripped-up chairs thrown onto the stage, bricks hurled, flying bottles and, during a concert in Germany, a brutal police charge into the audience.

It's not just the music, they insist, it's the totality of what they're doing. It's the attitude: 'Clothes are the way we do things'. After an era where a prophet claimed 'You are what you eat', we hear a scream announcing 'Like trousers like brain'. Brief, biting, a squeezed-out, curt, casual warning against the dangers of pretension and other disguises of the personality. Reality is crawling ever closer, so you might as well wear what you are and succumb to a narrowed straightness that won't betray you.

The Damned culled their name from old horror movies, portraying the feelings rife in an era of despair. They travel with a sound, manic in content, aspiring to super-sonic speed. Their pronounced acknowledgement of a goal named money has cast them in a somewhat singular mould in the world of Punk. Be that as it may, their stance is resoundingly iconoclastic as any emissaries of hell might well be.

A slicked-down, plastered synthetic-looking hairstyle caps a bent-over head. Long, sharpened fingernails, fat cigar, narrow slits for eyes seethe in smears of dark shadowed gloom. Turbulent names for turbulent times: Rat Cabies, Captain Sensible, anian. On stage, Rat Scabies pours lighter fuel onto his drum kit and sets light to it. anian wears vampiric costume, surrounded by swirl-ing dust clouds and waving arms. Other players dress in rag and monstrous relics of the absurd abound.

Their backgrounds include school drop-outs and jobs ranging from lavatory attendant to grave digger. They play till it hurts and only then begin to approach the threshold of satisfaction. Publicity photos reveal angry but blank faces like something off a Wanted poster. Prior to one gig they received champagne, flowers and lemon pies from the Rolling Stones. During the first set they flung the flowers into the audience. During the second they threw the pies. Their stage impact leaves the audience stunned, silent. Then after a moment there is a delayed response like an escape from a trauma.

Punk criticizes the Stranglers because of their background. They are all in their mid-twenties with musical roots stretching back to pub rock. Now superstars of the New Wave, they're accused of repacking their image to take advantage of present fashion trends. Lurk-ing hints of refinement and academic achievement add to the fuel of antagonism preva-lent amongst the predominantly working class Punk majority. That's all in the background. In the foreground they are unquestionably Punk.

Their energy is incredible, their beat fast and heavy. Their condemnation of the tradi-tional pitfalls of stardom is vehement. Their content touches what they feel many people forget and need reminding of. Their perceptions take voice in the seamy regions of dark domains, ranging from the sewers of London to other realms of living hell. *Ugly, Hanging Around, Down in the Sewer, Peasant in the Big Shitty* are some of the titles suggestive of their sentiment: they insist they want to be refreshingly different.

Rebelling against Mr Normal, the Jam escaped the world of establishment employ-ment: building trades and inspection. Jam means to play loose and enjoy music. That fitted their intentions and they named themselves accordingly.

Sound and content are undeniably Punk but their look is different. They wear suits on stage insisting they have the right. Their performance is laced with tension and aggres-sion which when mingled with the suited background seems as if it will never reach any point of release. Like many others they revere the concept of accessibility but in their case they refer only to the substance of the music and not to their situation or attitudes.

Sniffin' Glue, the first of the fanzines, attacked the Jam for taking an unnecessarily long time to tune up before playing. *Sniffin' Glue* got burnt, literally and symbolically, on stage while the group were tuning up. They disclaim judgements and established forms of criti-cism, urging the fans to experience without instruction from outsiders and seniors. They also stress a desire to be famous, and seem well on the way.

The root following of Punk probably only numbered a few hundred people. The spread of the movement has engulfed many thousands more, so how long the fresh, critical assault on society will survive is an open question. The most significant thing about the Punk movement is that nothing is definite and the aim is change—any change. How long will it be before the vital energy of the innovators is consumed by posing invaders? Visiting the clubs in the autumn of 1977, the atmosphere had certainly changed: older faces, Japanese tourists, gaping Parisians, German film crews. Has Punk moved on—or has it already become swallowed by the consuming sterility of the music business machine? The Sex Pistols: shattering voices in a plastic wilderness? A break-through in artistic awareness?

When the group started, they fitted no previous pattern of entertainment. Instead of a presentable image of glitter rock or tailored jazz, they were spiky teenagers, snarling and sneering, fresh from the gutters, draped in venom. They were so loud that every-one bounced and shook. It was a primal scream with a mesmerizing heaviness. Malcolm McClaren found the Pistols in his clothes shop 'Sex', in 1975. After an unsuc-cessful stint with the New York

Dolls he came back to the King's Road and combined an embryonic teenage rock group with a bored youth who hung about the shop and looked as if he might be a singer. Johnny became Rotten because Steve Jones said 'he never brushed his teeth and they used to be green'.

The content of their act, at first incoherent, slithered through, and from an indignant response emerged outrage. Audiences might tolerate biting insult or crude social realism from a safe distance, but the Pistols played at close quarters on a low level stage, without barriers. The audience could leave or pull the plugs out. The first gig lasted ten minutes and then the plugs were pulled. The second gig they got through a thirty minute set, before being asked to leave. More gigs followed and a response pattern began to emerge.

Indignation erupted and rooms, clubs and halls emptied with speeds hitherto unknown. But gradually some didn't run, some stayed. Those fans listened and they came back for more. They checked out the wheres and whens of the next Pistols performances and followed them from place to place. They persisted and out of them emerged a contingent of committed devotees —the germ of a movement.

The word spread and the nucleus of a Pistols fandom took root. Punk was spreading. Symbols of identification were being selected. The cheap safety pin snapped into place on clothes and more importantly on flesh. The fans displayed their individualism in dress and assembled themselves with the same consideration that possesses any stage-conscious artist.

The fanzine *Sniffin' Glue* got underway. In it the kids spoke for themselves to themselves. The format was immediate and cheap. It seethed with crude, uninhibited energy. The circulation began with sixty copies and quickly increased into hundreds. The content was insulting, brazen, attacking, and as unrestrained as the Pistols themselves. It was the antithesis of the dull sterility propagated by the established music press.

McLaren's next step forward was to launch the Pistols onto the fashionable 'Chelsea set'. They were engaged to perform at a party by Andrew Logan, a well-known artist/sculptor. The Pistols burst into life, doing their utmost to assault and insult. Jordan, fashion forerunner of Punkdom —adorned in bondage and with face and hair luridly multi—coloured —ended the evening being stripped on stage by Johnny Rotten.

The word was spreading. Some began to consider the Pistols as viable entertainment —and wherever they went fandom followed.

On February 20th 1976 the Pistols played as support band at the Marquee Club in Soho and got their first, non-committal review in the music press. Johnny marked the evening by throwing a chair at an amplifier. The Pistols were banned from the club and dismissed from a proposed tour. Then Viv Stanshall, late of the Bonzo Dog Band, broke his leg and the Pistols filled in at the Nashville, a seedy high-ceilinged cross between a pub and a frontier saloon whose usual offering was Country and Western. The Pistols were invited back.

Other bookings followed and on stage, rage and tantrums erupted, gigs ended with heavy theatrical violence, drums got kicked in and guitars smashed. Johnny Rotten began to be quoted in the music press—the first forays of Punk philosophy. Everyone could form a group like the Pistols. There was nothing patronizing in his advice. He was the antithesis of the unattainable superstar, exuding total reality, insisting it wasn't just enough to listen to him. The Pistols weren't leaders—at the most they were the first spokesmen for Punk feeling, nothing more. People had to think for themselves. Skill was an incidental quality that created no barriers. By July 1976 similar bands were starting up and Punk was spreading.

To the uninitiated and the older the spectacle of Punk mixed with the strident, uncompromising beat, provoked a tremendous fear. The voice of youth and discontent was growing stronger and smelt of rebellion. The relentless edge of chaos was ever present as the Pistols led the

way in a Punk festival at the 00 Club in Oxford Street. In September 1976 on the second night, the edge of chaos tipped over into disaster, although the Pistols weren't in. A glass was thrown, a girl was blinded and Punk was banned from the club. Newspapers, radio and TV began to catch on—the Pistols had become a dangerous cult and social threat. Personalities who had never seen or heard them attacked them for what they were assumed to be.

Things seemed to change when the giant record company EMI signed up the Pistols. Fandom accused the Pistols of selling out to the Rolls Royce Brigade. The Pistols denied any money-orientated motives. They were only striving to reach the widest possible audience. 'Here at last is a group with a lot of guts for younger people to identify with; a group that parents actually won't tolerate. And it's not just parents that need a little shaking up, it's the music business itself', remarked the A&R manager at EMI. But it didn't last. His statement rang a little too true.

The Pistols started recording. *Anarchy in the UK* was the first A side. *Sniffin' Glue* said it destroyed all rock'n'roll laws and kicked the establishment in the balls. McClaren said that it was a statement on self-rule. 'Great fuckin' record' said a Punk. 'What's Anarchy?'

On December 1st 1976 nascent anti-Pistol sentiment found a focal point to justify its antagonism. During the 'Today' programme, at peak viewing time on Thames Television, presenter Bill Grundy interviewed the Pistols live and sailed in, antagonistic and aggressive. Provoked but unrepentant, the Pistols used, among a few others, the words 'shit' and 'fuck'. Grundy was suspended for provoking the 'incident'; an outraged lorry driver was reported to have kicked in his new colour television set—a planned UK tour was cancelled—EMI packers went on strike, refusing to handle *Anarchy in the UK;* the BBC banned the playing of the record; the Press had a field-day with headlines like 'Punk? Call it Filthy Lucre', 'TV Fury Over Rock Cult Filth', 'Were the

Pistols Loaded?'

The Pistols flew off to a concert in Holland. Now vomit splattered the headlines. 'The group are the most revolting people I have ever seen'. commented an airline check-in girl. EMI terminated the Pistols' contract while they were out of the country, announcing that it was mutually agreed. Malcolm McClaren claimed otherwise but picked up the £20,000 severance fee.

Meanwhile *Anarchy in the UK* got into the charts and sold 55,000 copies after only five radio plays. In February 1977 Glen Matlock left the group and was replaced by Sid Vicious on bass—an old mate of Johnny's, they used to haunt the King's Road together in mutual discontent, hurling bricks at passing cars and getting thrown out of pubs for fighting.

In March of Jubilee Year the Pistols signed with A & M Records in a ceremony outside the gates of Buckingham Palace. They announced the release of a new single, *God Save the Queen.* The courtship with A & M had barely started before rumblings of disapproval began. Other artists objected to sharing the label with notorious punk rockers. Sid Vicious made headlines with punch-ups and A & M terminated the contract: 'The company will not be releasing any product from the group and has no further association with them.'

A bemused Malcolm received a cheque for £25,000. 'The Sex Pistols are like some contagious disease —untouchable', he told reporters. 'Promoters have

been our worst enemies really', he lamented as cancellations and bannings persisted.

Then the Pistols signed with Virgin Records. The third signing in six months. Here was a safer haven. *God Save the Queen* was set to be released on May 27th. On May 31st the BBC banned it and commercial radio followed suit. Even so, it was within days the most requested record on London's Capital Radio.

Meanwhile, in Malcolm's shop, *God Save the Queen* T-shirts shared shelves with bondage straps. In January 1977 he and Vivienne Westwood had revamped 'Sex' to become 'Seditionaries —Clothes for Heroes' decorated with huge photos of Dresden after the bombing.

God Save The Queen made number one on the New Musical Express chart, but blank spaces marked its ascendance up the BBC charts, where it was still banned.

Johnny Rotten got stabbed outside a North London pub. The next day Paul Cook got attacked in Shepherd's Bush and hit over the head with an iron bar. When he was asked what he thought the reasons might be, he replied: 'Loads . . . but that's London at the moment . . . it's a violent town . . . it's easy for a gang to pick on one person and get his head smashed in'.

The next release, *Pretty Vacant*, was accepted by the BBC. Capital Radio did a two-hour interview with Johnny to prove that the 'foul-mouthed' Pistol did show hints of normality. Pressured between fame and notoriety Malcolm McClaren found it impossible to get gigs, so the Pistols scoured the countryside using assumed names, appearing at small venues, keeping in contact with the fans.

Problems continued to dog their recording efforts. Their third single *Holidays in the Sun* was released in October and reached Number 6 in the charts, but there were problems with a Belgian Travel Agency over the copyright of the sleeve. The long awaited album *Never Mind the Bollocks, Here's The Sex Pistols* was finally released on October 28th and made Number 1 four weeks later. Again there were problems, this time over the poster advertising the album, and a number of record shops were prosecuted, charged with indecent display. The offending word? *Bollocks*. The first case was heard in Nottingham, with John Mortimer defending. A Professor of English defined the word 'bollocks' as meaning 'nonsense'. Case dismissed.

Since early summer Malcolm had been setting up a feature film starring the Sex Pistols to be directed by Russ 'Super-Vixen' Meyer. The working title for the film was *Who killed Bambi?* After many false starts and problems with the backers, the film ground to a halt in late November. The Pistols returned to playing.

They flew to Holland for a two week tour, returning in mid-December to play a number of unadvertised gigs, including one on Christmas Day. Fandom was temporarily appeased.

1978—a new year and a US tour. They departed in Januar after inevitable hassles over visas. Malcolm had chosen to avoid the usual rock venues and the tour kicked off in Atlanta, Georgia. On to Memphis, Randy's Rodeo in San Antonio (where there was a minor riot), Baton Rouge, Dallas (where a member of th audience spat in Sid's face, who retaliated by hitting the offender over the head with hi guitar), Tulsa, then finally on t San Francisco for the last concert of the tour. It really was the Sex Pistols' last and final gig. For it was in San Francisco that the band broke up.

There had been reports of discontent among the group for some time, that the film had kept them from playing, that no new songs had been written since *Bodies*, there was criticism of Sid's drug involvement, and of Johnny's bodyguards. The band were due to fly down to Rio to meet up with Ronald Biggs, 'the great train robber', but there was a row, the culmination of months of general malaise. The net result was John flying off to New York to stay with friends, Sid overdosing on a plane to New York a few days later, and Paul and Steve, after a few days in LA, flying down to Rio to join Biggs.

The initial reaction to the break-up was that it would only be temporary but when John returned to England he gave an interview and made it quite clear: 'I won't work again with any of them, and that's no great pity. I'm bored chronic of singing the same set we'd played for two years. I'm looking for a new band, but I don't want to do no Johnny Rotten show again. I hated that in the Sex Pistols.'

So the Sex Pistols, who epitomized Punk, like Punk have moved on. Johnny and Sid are both, separately in search of new musicians, while Paul and Steve have been down in Rio enjoying Mister Biggs's company and there's talk of them making a record together.

At least they died before they got old . . .

IAN RAKOFF

PISTOLS

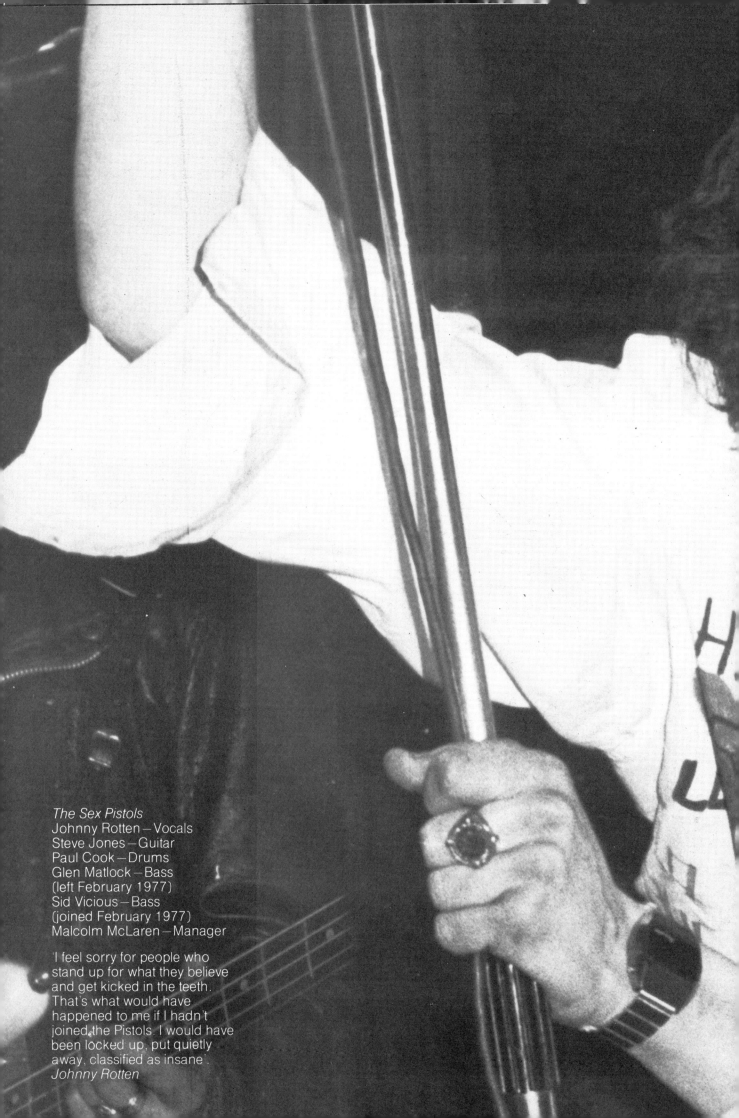

The Sex Pistols
Johnny Rotten — Vocals
Steve Jones — Guitar
Paul Cook — Drums
Glen Matlock — Bass
(left February 1977)
Sid Vicious — Bass
(joined February 1977)
Malcolm McLaren — Manager

'I feel sorry for people who
stand up for what they believe
and get kicked in the teeth.
That's what would have
happened to me if I hadn't
joined the Pistols. I would have
been locked up, put quietly
away, classified as insane'.
Johnny Rotten

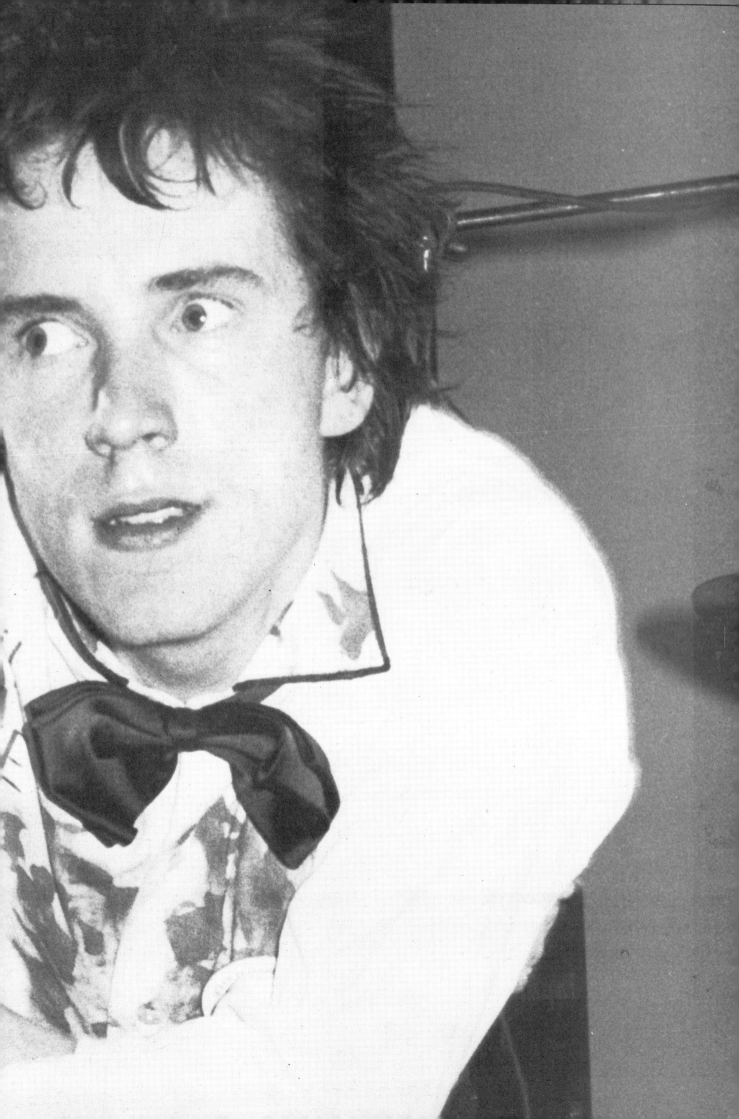

'A quartet of spiky teenage misfits from the wrong end of various London roads, playing 60s style white Punk rock'. *Neil Spenser, New Musical Express*

'We have to fight the entire super band system . . . They have nothing to offer the kids any more'. *Johnny Rotten*

'You can get whatever you want. It's called effort. It doesn't take much, just a lot of guts'. *Johnny Rotten*

'The Sex Pistols are a force. You get that feeling from their audience and it sticks in your mind. The clothes, the hair, and even the attitude of the audience has a direct link with the band'. *Mark P., Sniffin' Glue, October 1976*

'The Pistols are presenting one alternative to apathy and if you don't like it that's just too bad. It's not political anarchy . . . It's musical anarchy'. *Johnny Rotten*

In November 1976, EMI released the Sex Pistols' first single *Anarchy in the UK/I Wanna Be Me.*

Anarchy in the UK
Right now! I'm an Anti-Christ
I am an anarchist.
Don't know what I want but I
   know where to get it
I wanna destroy passers-by
Because I wanna be Anarchy
No dog's body!

Anarchy for the UK
It's coming sometime, maybe.
Give the wrong time
Stop a traffic line
Your future dream is a
   shopping scheme
'Cause I wanna be Anarchy in
   the city.
(© *The Sex Pistols 1976)*

'Anarchy in the UK is a statement of self-rule'. *Malcolm McLaren*

'This single destroys all the rock'n'roll laws'. *Mark P.*

n 9th October 1976, eleven
onths after their first
erformance, the Sex Pistols
gned with EMI.
think they're a rare breed of
tist. They're total
itertainment and in a lot of
ays uncompromising in what
ey want to do . . . If they
n't make it, then there's no
ture in rock'n'roll'. *Nick
bbs, A&R, EMI*

e're the best, we wouldn't
ve signed with a crackpot
e company. Now we can't
ignored'. *Johnny Rotten*

'I have never believed the national press and I'm surprised a lot of people did. The gullibility of the British public is excessive'. *Johnny Rotten*

On December 1st 1976 the Sex Pistols appeared live on the Thames Television *Today* programme, interviewed by Bill Grundy—below is an excerpt from this programme.

Grundy: I am told you have received £400 from a record company. Doesn't that seem slightly opposed to an anti-materialistic way of life?
Pistol: The more the merrier.
Grundy: Tell me more.
Pistol: Fuckin' spent it, didn't we?

Grundy: You're serious? Beethoven, Mozart, Bach?
Pistol (sarcastically): They're wonderful people, they really turn us on.
Grundy: Suppose they turn other people on?
Pistol (whispering): That's just their tough shit.
Grundy: It's what?
Pistol: Nothing, a rude word.
Grundy: No, no. What was the rude word?
Pistol: Shit.
Grundy: Was it really? Good heavens (to some girls who have accompanied the Pistols) What about the girls behind? Are you married or just enjoying yourselves?
Girl: I've always wanted to meet you.
Grundy: Did you really? We'll meet afterwards, shall we?
Pistol: You dirty old man.
Grundy: Go on. You've got a long time yet. You've got another five seconds. Say something outrageous.
Pistol: You dirty fucker. What a fuckin' rotter.
Grundy (to the audience): Well, that's it for tonight. I'll be seeing you soon'(turns to Pistols) I hope I'm not seeing you again.

The interviews resulted in the national press launching the Sex Pistols on the British public the following day with 'Shock Horror' headlines . . .

the punks

OBNOXIOUS!
OUTRAGEOUS!

PUNK ROC

NK

ROTTEN

CK

RAZORED

BILEE

ROCK GROUP START A
4-LETTER
TV STORM

OCK

OCKER

WERE THE
PISTOLS
LOADED?

PUNKY PAM
She was on TV last year . . .
"and that was pretty wild, too."

Rock Horror Show

Punk Rock group 'plied with booze'

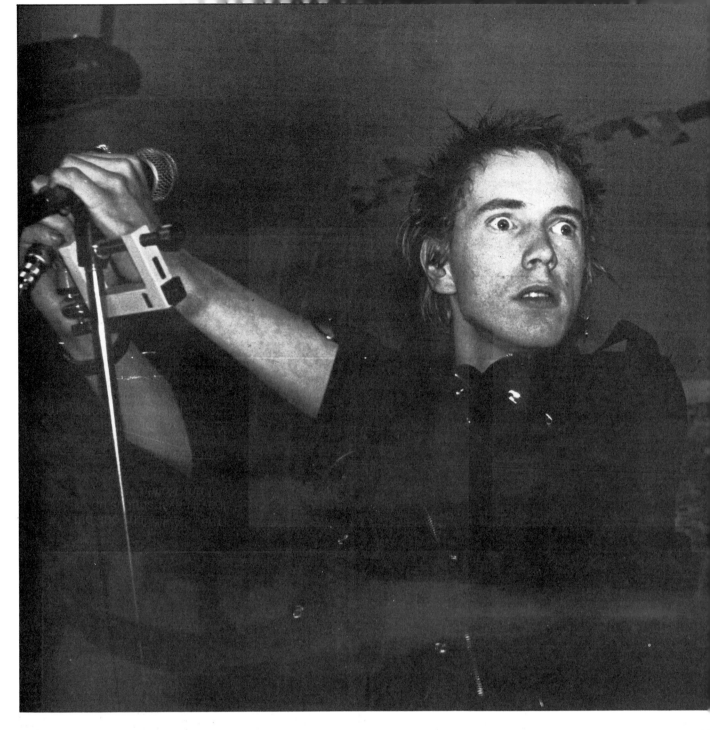

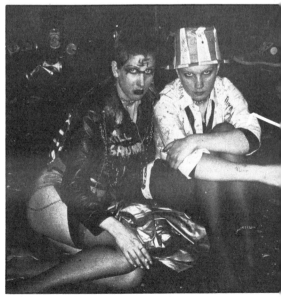

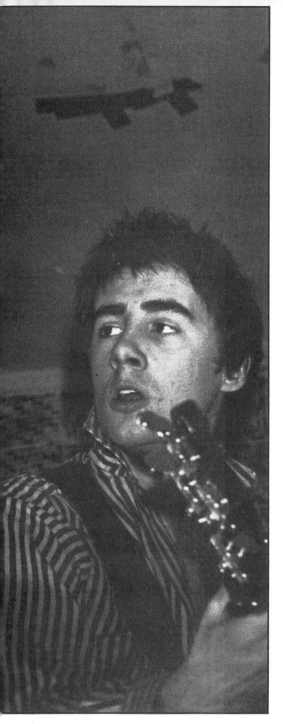

On 3rd December the Anarchy Tour on which the Pistols were supported by the Clash, the Damned and the Heartbreakers, took to the road, but as a result of all the adverse publicity they played only six of the twenty-five dates booked.

'That was soul-destroying. We thought we were the greatest rock and roll bands, conquering the world . . . everyone got really excited but the day before the tour started the Grundy thing happened and gigs started being cancelled. The Pistols suffered quite terribly, it was really tragic . . .' *Mick Jones, The Clash*

'I don't see why councillors should dictate to people what kids go out and listen to any night . . . it's up to the kids, who work and pay taxes just like anyone else, to decide what they want to do. I'm just sick of the whole thing. We feel like a bunch of prisoners'. *Johnny Rotten*

'At our gig in Caerphilly this priest shouted out that God could forgive anyone — even murderers! But not punk rockers, they were the devil's children'. *Johnny Rotten*

On January 20th 1977 after much rumbling, EMI terminated their contract with the Pistols.
'If we walk into another record company what are they going to say? "If you can't play anywhere and we can't hear your records on the radio and EMI decides to drop you . . ." What the hell are they going to do?' *Malcolm McLaren*

Rotten to the Core
1st Issue — January 1977
Nottingham
'I want to put the Sex Pistols on the front of every issue. It's named after Johnny Rotten, they started it all, they made it all possible'. *Dave Chaos (18)*

In February bassist Glen Matlock left the Pistols and was replaced by Sid Vicious, an old friend of Johnny's. 'I don't understand why people think it's so difficult to learn to play the guitar. I found it incredibly easy. You just pick a chord, go twang, and you've got Music'. *Sid Vicious*

On March 10th the Pistols signed with A & M Records. 'Their behaviour has never offended me. I find them refreshing and exciting'. *Derek Green, A & M Records*

Six days later the contract was terminated. Derek Green was later to say 'The Sex Pistols were the quickest success I ever had. They played me eight songs which really knocked me out and I signed them pig-headedly'.

'There's no compromise; a record company is there to market records, not to dictate terms. I'm not going to be dictated to by some little recording company Hitler'. *Johnny Rotten*

'I keep walking in and out of offices being given cheques . . . it's crazy'. *Malcolm McLaren*

Virtually banned from playing in England, a world tour cancelled, and with no record company, the Pistols performed in April before an invited audience at the Screen on the Green cinema.

'But we don't need any sympathy and we ain't martyrs. Martyrs are failures. We ain't failures 'cos we never give up'. *Johnny Rotten*

On May 12th the Pistols signed with Virgin Records. 'We think they are just the band for an independent record label like Virgin, which is answerable to itself and the public only . . . the Sex Pistols have thrown a very successful spanner into the rock works. They have stirred up the industry. It is thanks almost entirely to them that many new wave bands have been abe to emerge at all'. *Richard Branson, Virgin Records*

On May 27th their second single *God Save The Queen* was released. It was banned after only four days' airplay but it made number one in the *New Musical Express* charts on 11th June.

God Save the Queen
God save the Queen
The fascist regime
It made you a moron
A potential H bomb

God save the Queen
She ain't no human being
There is no future
In England's dreaming
(© *The Sex Pistols 1977*)

'The single is nothing personal against the Queen, it's what she stands for . . . a symbol'. *Johnny Rotten*

TOP 20 POPS

FIRST CUT IS THE DEEPEST	ROD STEWART
LUCILLE	KENNY ROGERS
EVERGREEN	BARBRA STREISAND
AIN'T GONNA BUMP NO MORE	JOE TEX
SHOW YOU THE WAY TO GO	JACKSONS
YOU'RE MOVING OUT TODAY	CAROLE BAYER SAGER
THE SHUFFLE	VAN MCCOY
GOOD MORNING JUDGE	10CC
HALF WAY DOWN THE STAIRS	M
GOT TO GIVE IT UP	MAR
O.K.	ROC
TELEPHONE LINE	
LIDO SHUFFLE	
TOKYO JOE	
DISCO INFERNO	
TOO HOT TO HANDLE	
GONNA CAPTURE YOUR HEART	
WE CAN DO IT	
MAH NA MAH NA	

RECORD TOKENS
On Sale only at
the Customer
Service Counter

& Tape

'They can shut us out, but they'll never shut us up'.
Johnny Rotten

Pretty Vacant
Don't ask us to pretend
'Cos we're not all there,
Don't pretend 'cos I don't care,
Don't need evolution,
Too much is real,
Stop your cheap comment
'Cos we know what we feel.

'Cos we're so pretty
Oh so pretty vacant
And we don't care.
(©*The Sex Pistols 1977*)

'Anyone can enjoy our music now'. *Johnny Rotten*

31

Viva La Resistance
1st Issue — February 1977
Preston
'The fanzine just happened
one boring Sunday afternoon.
. . The name. . sums up our
resistance against apathy and
the state of things today, punk
rock for me is a 24 hour
occupation…I listen to nothing
else, I talk about nothing
else…I believe it's the greatest
thing youth has ever
produced.' *Roy* (18)

The **NEW WAVE** magazine

New Wave
1st Issue — January 1977
Barnet, Herts
'As a magazine we try to differ
from the others . . . We try to
be energetic, spontaneous,
and original . . . We include
comments, poems . . . We
aren't interested in fashion, but
in new music by new bands.
We work. We don't live off the
dole. We don't want to be kept
alive by hand-outs from the
state . . .' *Ade*

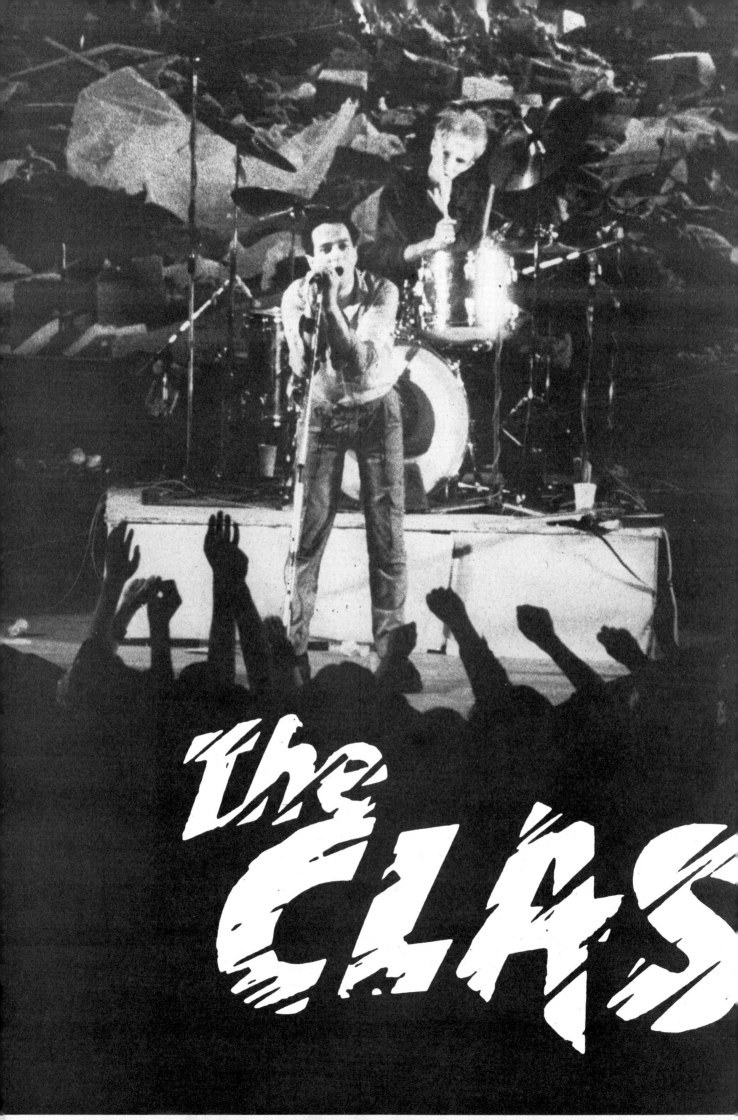

The Clash
Joe Strummer — Vocals/guitar
Mick Jones — Vocals/guitar
Paul Simenon — Bass
Terry Chimes — Drums
(left March 1977)
Mick Headdon — Drums
(joined April 1977)

'Just think about who's doing
what and what you're going to
do about it, is all we're saying,
"think for yourself"!' *Joe
Strummer*

'I think people have got to find
out where their directions lie
and channel their violence into
music, or something creative'.
Mick Jones

White Riot
All the power is in the hands,
Of people rich enough
to buy it,
While we walk the streets,
Too chicken to even try it,
And everybody does what
   they're told to,
And everybody eats
   supermarket soul-food,
White riot, I wanna riot!
White riot, a riot of me own.

White riot! I wanna riot,
White riot! A riot of me own!
(Strummer/Jones)

1977
In 1977,
I hope to go to heaven,
Been too long on the dole,
Now I can't work at all,
Danger stranger,
You better paint your face,
No Elvis, Beatles or the Rolling
    Stones,

In 1977,
Knives in W11,
Ain't so lucky to be rich,
Sten guns in Knightsbridge,
Danger stranger,
You better paint your face,
No Elvis, Beatles or the Rolling
    Stones,
(Strummer/Jones)

'It only takes an hour to write a
song . . . you can play
anything inside three weeks'.
Joe Strummer

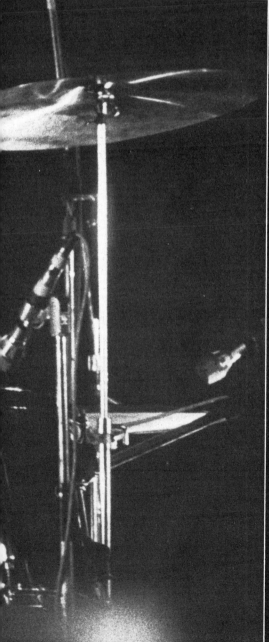

'We're supposed to be a shout from the gutter, right?' *Joe Strummer*

'People say our songs are political now because we deal in things that affect daily life, but I ain't got no major plan to change the world'. *Joe Strummer*

'It's a clash against things that are going on . . . the music scene and all that. We're hoping to change quite a lot'. *Paul Simenon*

London's Burning
1st Issue—January 1977
London
'The fanzine by a Clash fan for Clash fans, has been done because it beats sharpening pencils'. *Jonh Ingham* (25)

e are not top of the political ps. We are not the new ders that everyone seems be searching for'. *Mick nes*

m not interested in singing out love and kisses . . . I'm terested in why? Why I can't this or that. Why?' *Joe rummer*

Live Wire
1st Issue—January 1977
London
'I got interested when I used to go to the 100 club and the Hope and Anchor in the early days. It was amazing watching the Pistols and the Damned with loads of energy. It was great that they behaved like human beings and you could talk to them afterwards—not like being miles away from Rod Stewart or the Stones and then watching them ride off in their limousines. I intend to keep the mag going mainly for small bands who never get a look in . . . If you don't like *Live Wire* don't just throw it away, write in and better it yourself . . .' *Alan Anger*

THE DAMNED

The Damned
Dave Vanian — Vocals
Brian James — Guitar
Captain Sensible — Bass
Rat Scabies — Drums
(left October 1977)

'In the last few years I've got
really pissed off with the guys
who just get on stage and
don't even look as if they're
into what they're doing. It's like
a job to them and they might
as well be sitting in a factory'.
Brian James

'I don't draw on any rock star
to help my performance, I
have more affinity to camp
horror movies'. *Dave Vanian*

Neat, Neat, Neat
No crime if there ain't no law,
No more cops left to mess you
    round,
No more dreams of mystery
    chords,
No more sight to bring you
    down,
Got a crazy got a thought my
    mind,
My minds on when she falls
    asleep,
Feeling fine in her restless
    time
When come these words upon
    me creep:
Neat, neat, neat — she can't
    afford no cannon,
Neat, neat, neat — she can't
    afford no gun at all,
Neat, neat, neat — she can't
    afford no cannon,
Neat, neat, neat — she ain't
    got no name to call
(Brian James)

'What about the 16 year old kid on the streets who ain't got no life, they're the ones we're going for'. *Rat Scabies*

'We get stunned reaction right! . . . we've got to stamp out boredom'. *Captain Sensible*

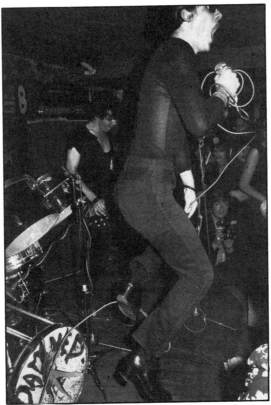

Ripped & Torn
1st Issue—November 1976
Glasgow
'Already you can hear the shrieks of the old rich as they finally realise they've been made redundant by the energy-ridden bands who work out of necessity in cheap clubs with lousy P.A.'s. That's Rock and Roll'. *Tony D.*

'Our music is intense because it comes from inside us and we want to let it out. I suppose as society gets tougher the music gets tougher, too'. *Brian James*

Sideburns/Strangled
1st Issue: January 1977
London
'1976—year of change—Sex
Pistols, Damned . . . kids start
to rebel against the hype/big
business in the only way they
can—tear down Earls Court—
Led Zeppelin etc. Music
returns to the streets . . .'
T. Moon

SHEWS

Shews—London
'Boredom, Denied, Used,
Cheated, Manipulated,
Ignored—this is what happens
to the Youth—the future of
Britain. We were so depressed
that even starting a group
wouldn't have been enough.
This is where *Shews* began . . .'
Pete

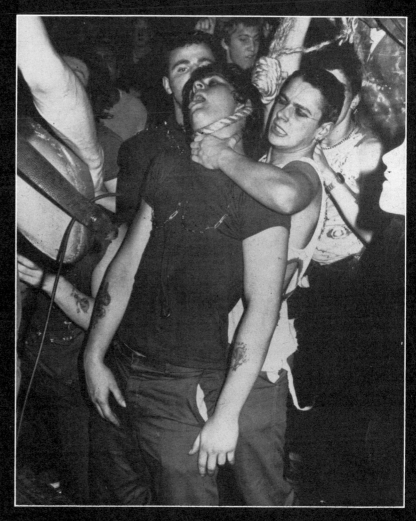

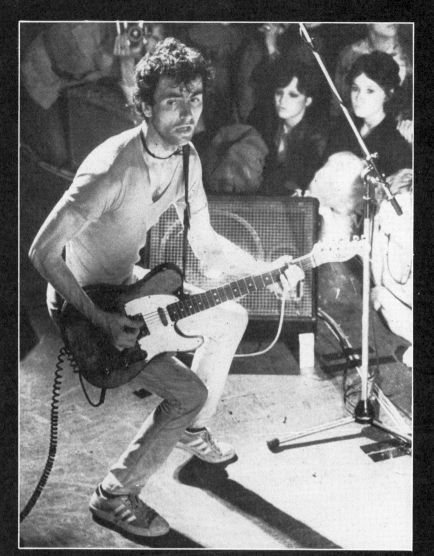

The Stranglers
Hugh Cornwell—Vocals/guitar
Jean Jacques Burnel—
    Bass/vocals
Dave Greenfield—Keyboards
Jet Black—Drums

'We're playing aggressive music that's attacking people's heads. The more broad-minded you are, the better'. *Hugh Cornwell*

'There's definitely a lot of new bands who've got a lot of energy . . . and there's a whole new mood, rock'n'roll's folk music, y'know, so there is a "new wave" and we are part of it'. *J.J.*

'There's nothing new in swearing on stage. The comedians have been doing it around the clubs for years . . . I wish Lenny Bruce was still around, he'd love all this . . .' *Hugh Cornwell*

the stranglers

Get a Grip on Yourself
Didn't have the money round
   to buy a 'Morry thou'
Been around and seen a lot
   to shake me anyhow.
Begged and borrowed some-
   times,
I admit I even stole
The worst crime that I ever
   did was playin' Rock and Roll

But the money's no good. Just
   get a grip on yourself
But the money's no good. Just
   get a grip on yourself

Suffering convictions on a two-
   way stretch inside
The air in here is pretty thin,
   I think I'll go outside.
Committed for insanity and
   crimes against the soul
The worst crime that I ever did
   was play some Rock and Roll
*(©1977 April Music Ltd/Albion
Music Ltd)*

'I think people are very scared
of the unknown, in fact, even
when it comes down to music
a lot of people are scared to sit
and listen to music they don't
understand. They have a
music complex in a way . . .'
Jet Black

'We've never pretended to be younger than we are, we've never tried to play faster than we do'. *J.J.*

'That's what the artist is for, to make people's directions change. He asks questions about everything . . . so the punk "new wave" bands are asking questions about music and its relevance to life today'. *Hugh Cornwell*

Skum
1st Issue — February 1977
London
'Sept-Dec '76. — After
becoming disillusioned with
my heroes, Elton John & The
Who, I started frequenting
Rock On record shop in
search of accessible music.
Met Mark P. . . & bought a
copy of S. G. 4 with the Clash
in it. I was inspired by what
Mark had to say.' Rick (15)

Cliché
1st Issue—April 1977
'We are not offering opinions, which are of no interest to anyone except the author, but plain facts, a little insight, and information gleaned from personal contact with the musicians . . . Music lasts, fashion doesn't'. *Tim (19)*

The Jam

The Jam
Paul Weller—Vocals/guitar
Bruce Foxton—Bass
Rick Buckler—Drums

'The whole thing about the
New Wave was that it went
against the old rules . . . That's
really what Punk Rock, New
Wave, call it what you will, is all
about—accessibility'. *Paul
Weller*

'I didn't want to go to work. I
didn't want to be Mr Normal'.
Paul Weller

In the City
In the city, there's a thousand
    things I wanna say to you,
In the city, there's a thousand
    faces all shining bright
And those golden faces are
    under 25
They wanna say, they wanna
    tell you
About their young ideas
You better listen now, you said
    your bit.
(Weller)

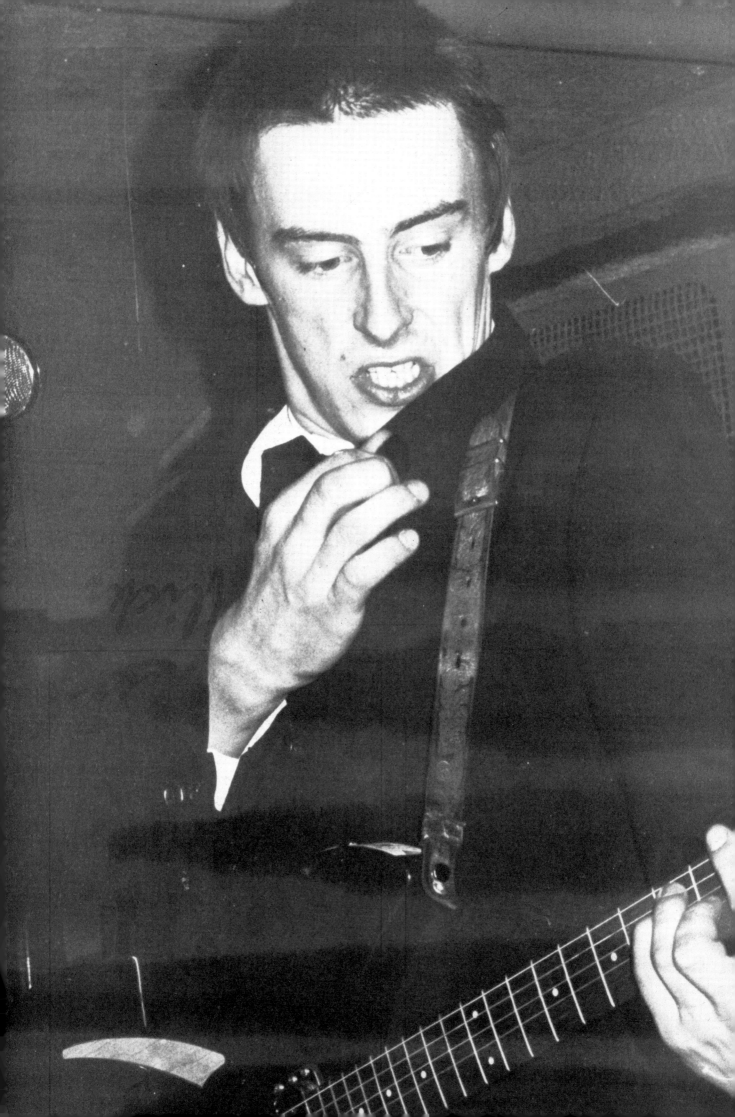

All Around the World
All over the country
Want a new direction
I said all over this land
A new reaction
Well, there has to be a youth
    explosion
A re-creation
For something we can
    command.

What's the point of saying
    destroy
I want a new life for everyone
All around the world I been
    looking for new
All around the world I been
    looking for new
Youth Explosion!!
(Weller)

Time for Truth
What you trying to say that
    you haven't tried to say
    before,
You're just another red
    balloon with a lot of hot gas,
Why don't you fuck off.

And you think you got us
    sussed out,
And you think that we're
    brainwashed,
And you're trying for a
    police state,
So you can rule our bodies
    and our minds.

I bet you sleep at night in silk
    sheets and a clean mind,
Whilst killers roam the streets
    in numbers dressed in blue.
(Weller)

'All we're into reviving, and all
the bands are into reviving, is
accessible music'. *Paul Weller*

'I'm not a prolific song writer. I write a song about once a month, but they're good and that's better than ten shitty ones'. *Paul Weller*

'We want to play as near perfect as possible. Even though the audience won't probably notice . . . we also want to play as loud as possible'. *Rick Buckler*

'What's happening in Parliament doesn't mean a lot to the average bloke. He just wants what's best for himself. We write about everyday things—it's a realistic message'. *Rick Buckler*

'We wear suits because we want to not because someone told us to. Our fortune is good fame, fortune and be recognized. We want to be famous. Everyone does and we'd be liars if we said we didn't'. *Paul Weller*

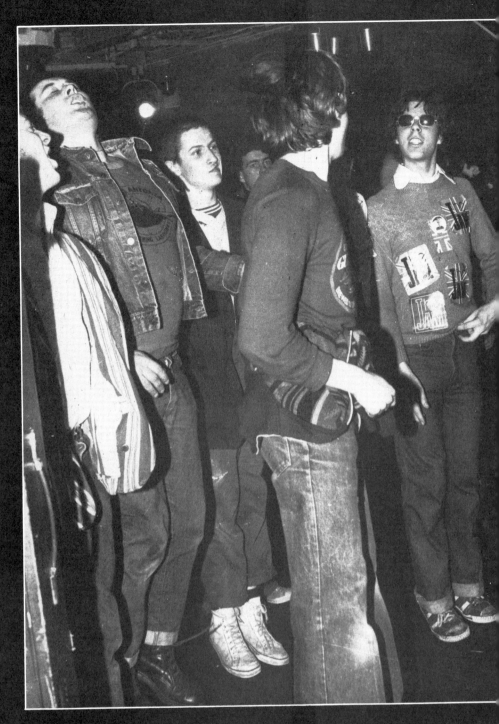

THESE THINC'S

These Things
1st Issue — November 1976
Ilford, Kent
'I'm seventeen years old and haven't got one qualification at all. In my opinion, "they" do not determine the level of your intelligence correctly . . . you can be on the lowest social level and have the most important asset . . . *common sense*, or you can have every piece of paper in the world and be the thickest, most bigheaded dunderbag on this planet . . .' *Arcane Vendetta*

flicks

Flicks
1st Issue—January 1977
London
'It's not only concerned with music, New Wave goes much further. It involves us all. Age doesn't mean a shit. No posing—Punk Rock does not mean razors, pins and more importantly swastikas . . .
Flicks, the title, the size — all to do with being a small booklet .
. . . keep flicking thru . . .' *Glen*

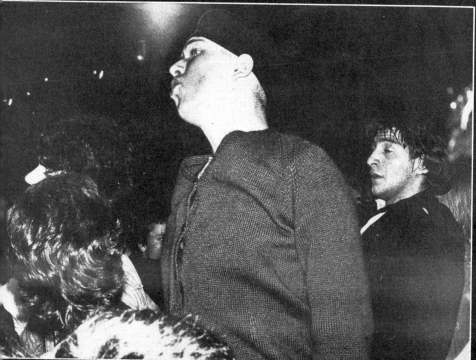

CHELSEA

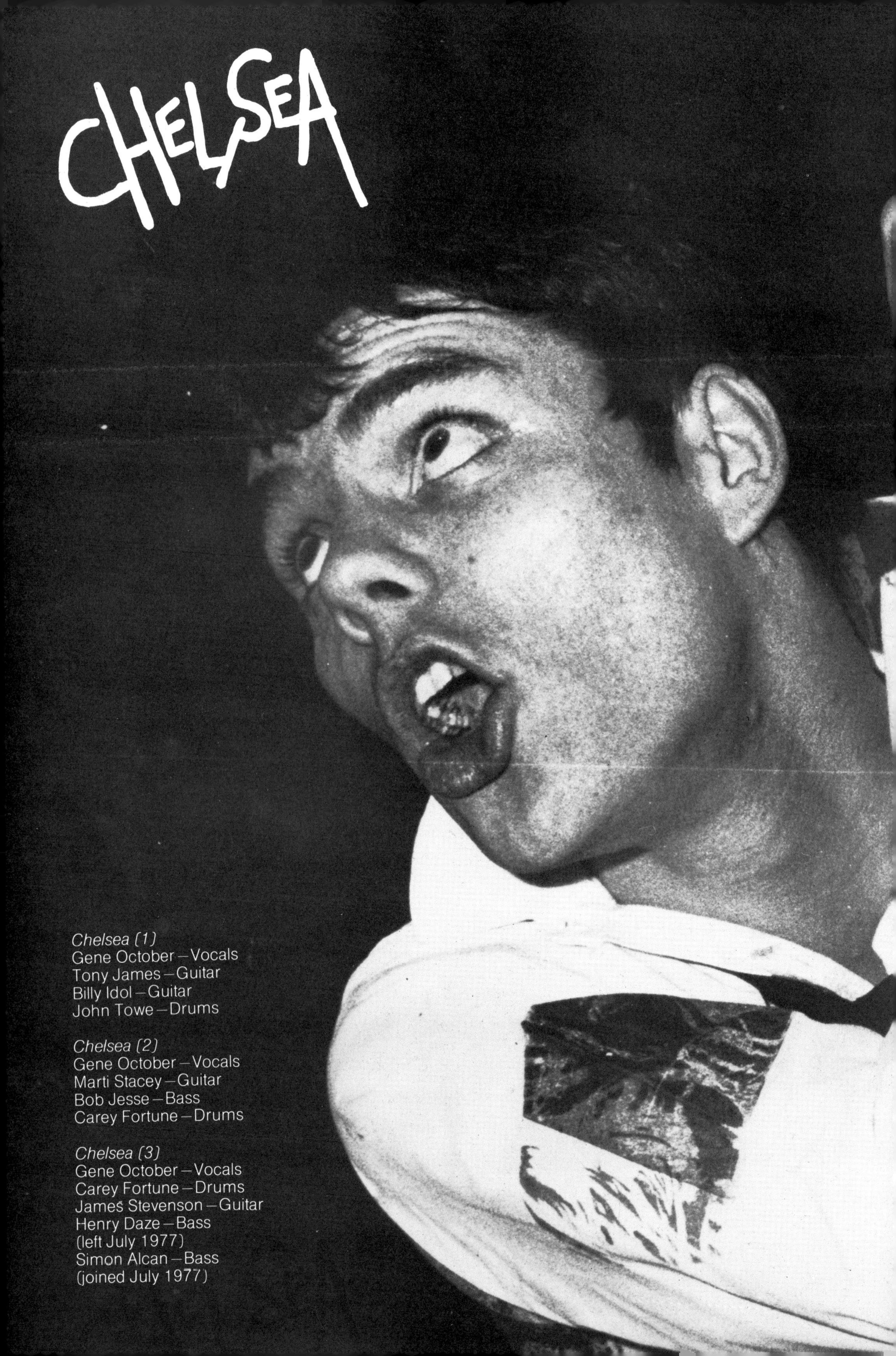

Chelsea (1)
Gene October — Vocals
Tony James — Guitar
Billy Idol — Guitar
John Towe — Drums

Chelsea (2)
Gene October — Vocals
Marti Stacey — Guitar
Bob Jesse — Bass
Carey Fortune — Drums

Chelsea (3)
Gene October — Vocals
Carey Fortune — Drums
James Stevenson — Guitar
Henry Daze — Bass
(left July 1977)
Simon Alcan — Bass
(joined July 1977)

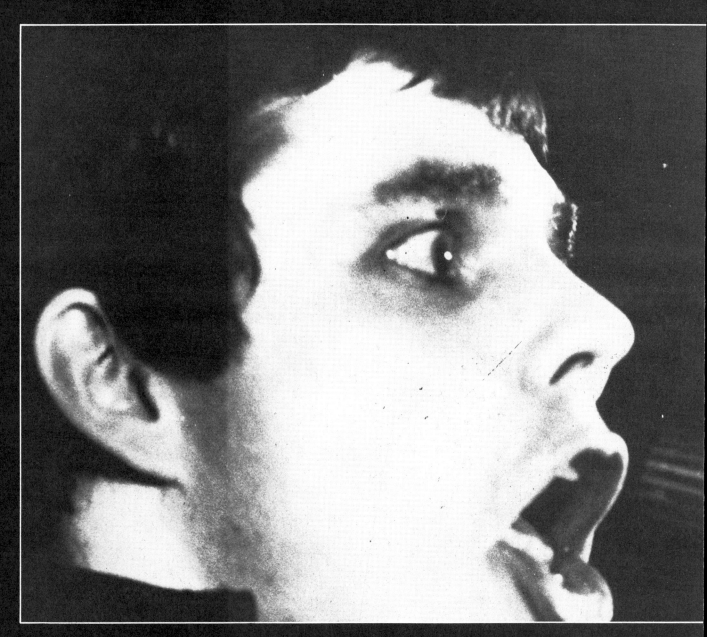

'Rock comes from a dirty old playground, in the slums, or the World's End, Chelsea'. *Gene October*

'Some of my songs are about my problems, some are about problems in general'. *Gene October*

'We're a generation that hasn't been through a war. I suppose you could say New Wave music is our personal war'. *Gene October*

'Everyone thinks that kids of the seventies are a useless generation. They think the kids are apathetic and parasitic, but that ain't true, because the New Wave is positive proof to the contrary'. *Chelsea (3)*

Right to Work
Standing around
For just seven days a week
I don't even get no signing-on
    fee,
I feel ripped off, yeah,
How about you?
Why was I born?
What are we gonna do?
'Cos we have the right to work,
'Cos we have the right to work,
Yes we do

I don't even know what
    tomorrow night brings
Let me tell ya
Having no future is a terrible
    thing,
Standing around waiting for
    our caviar
I don't take drugs
I don't drink beer
We have the right to work
We have the right to work
We have the right to work.
(October)

Right to Work means self
expression and the right to
choose. You don't have to do
what you're told . . . I don't
want the kids to look back and
say "1977, oh yeah, it was
great but what did they
achieve".' *Gene October*

48 Thrills
1st Issue – November 1976
Stevenage
'I do the mag because it's enjoyable writing, gives a feeling of involvement and a chance to say exactly what I feel.' *Adrian* (18)

MAY 77

NOT SUITABLE FOR ADULTS
A FANZINE FROM MANCHESTER

No 3

y Talk

t Issue—March 1977
anchester

July 1976 I was knocking
ound with a few Bowie/Roxy
aks. They were going to see

Slaughter and the Dogs . . .
also on the same bill were the
Buzzcocks and the Sex
Pistols. It was exciting, raw,
funny. I knew straight away it
was for me, it was the first time
I'd really got into anything'.
Steve

GENER

ATION X

Generation X
Billy Idol—Vocals
Tony James—Guitar
Bob Andrews—Bass
John Towe—Drums
(left April 1977)
Mark Laff—Drums
(joined June 1977)

'I feel we are aggressive, but in our playing . . . We want to convince through our songs. We're just a soft fist really'. *Tony James*

'It's really meant to be like Generation Positive—a positive reaction as opposed to a negative one'. *Tony James*

Your Generation
It might take a bit of violence
But violence ain't our only
   stance
It might make our friends
   enemies
But we gotta take that chance,
Ain't no time for substitutes,
Ain't no time for idle threats
Action's rather hard to please
'Cos what you give is what you
   get.
Your generation don't mean a
   thing to me.
(Idol/James)

'*Your Generation* is about forgetting the previous generation. Punk rock is trying to do that'. *Billy Idol*

'All the songs we write, we don't sit down thinking we'll write about politics or mining disasters. They are just spontaneous'. *Tony James*

'I went straight into a band from the front of a mirror where I posed rock'n'roll star style'. *Billy Idol*

'Our politics is — we say what we think, we do what we want and we play by nobody's rules — we don't play by the Punk Rock rules'. *Tony James*

Day by Day
Trapped inside a jungle
Locked inside the tube
Hate your next door neighbour
'Cos he's got more than you
Going round and round
Day by day
On the circle line
Round and round.
(Idol/James)

Buzzcocks
Howard Devoto—Vocals
(left February 1977)
Pete Shelley—Lead guitar/
vocals
Steve Diggle—Rhythm
John Maher—Drums
Garth—Bass
(joined February 1977, left
October 1977)
Steve Harvey—Bass
(joined November 1977)

'I formed the Buzzcocks
because I wanted to get
across what I was saying in the
market place, not in a small
office in a tower block. People,
I wanted people to hear. A lot
of what the Buzzcocks tried to
do in the early days was to
inspire'. *Howard Devoto*

Boredom
Now there's nothing behind
    me,
And I'm already a has-been,
My future ain't what it was,
I think I know the words that I
    mean.

You know me—I'm acting
    dumb,
You know the scene—very
    humdrum,
Boredom — boredom —
    boredom.
(Devoto/Shelley)

Breakdown
Oh mum can I grow outta,
What's a little too big for me,
I'm gonna give up that ghost,
Before it gives up me,
I wander loaded as a crowd,
A nowherewolf of pain,
Living next to nothing,
But my nevermind remains,
I gotta breakdown yeah, I'm
    gonna breakdown,
You gimme breakdown, yeah.
(Devoto / Shelley)

buzzcocks

Stranded
1st Issue—March 1977
Exeter, Devon
'I believe in Punk Rock. That's
why I want to write about it.
But these days, it's not so
much a case of telling people
about it, but telling them the
truth about it. The stuff in the
national press is like a 35p
novel, cheap, sensational
trash, great for a laugh but
bearing *no* resemblance to
reality'. *John Jacques*

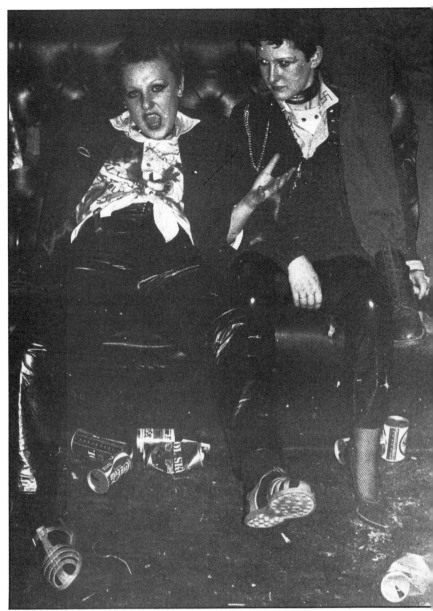

New Pose
1st Issue — May 1977
Leeds
'This magazine is dedicated to
the "Rock & Roll madness"
comic. Parts of which are
beginning to come true!'
Martin

THE SLITS

The Slits
Arri Up—Vocals
Tessa—Guitar
Palmolive—Drums
Kate Korus—Rhythm guitar
(left April 1977)
Viv Albertine—Rhythm guitar
(joined April 1977)

More On
1st Issue—London
'We began *More On* because we wanted to get "involved". The whole feeling at the time was that you had to do something. We felt something special, part of a new thing which was very radical — underground . . . We wanted (still do) really to be the ones on the stage . . . *More On* number one was done in two hours at school one afternoon . . .' *Sarah*

. . . They think only boys can play rock. That's why there aren't any girl groups. They don't push themselves'. *Arri Up*

'We have all got strong egos but it works out . . . I don't want to be in an orchestra. I've got my personality and I'm showing it on the stage. That's why I'm playing drums. I'm expressing myself and I want people to notice that'. *Palmolive*

'We always get a few people who are going "get 'em off" . . . We don't get dead quiet audiences . . . good atmospheres'. *The Slits*

'All the songs are really about ordinary things. The first one is called *Let's do the Split.* It's about guys who split up with us. It's like a typical guy who wants to have the woman under his thumb, like his housewife and all that. We're not having that'. *Arri Up*

Number One Enemy
If you like white, I'll be black,
If you like black, I'll be yellow,
If you like rational, I'll be
   impossible,
If you like reasonable, I'll be
   insane.
If you like peace and flowers,
I'm going to carry knives and
   chains.

I'm going to be your Number
   One Enemy,
All for the hell of it.
(Palmolive/Arri Up)

Love and Romance
I'm so happy,
You're so nice
Kiss kiss kiss
Fun fun life
Oh oh oh sweet love and
   romance.
(Viv Albertine)

'*Number One Enemy* is about all the people who tell you what to do all the time and you're just saying "fuck off" we're not having it! Then *Love and Romance* is a piss-take about lovey-dovey, kiss-kiss-kiss'. *Palmolive*

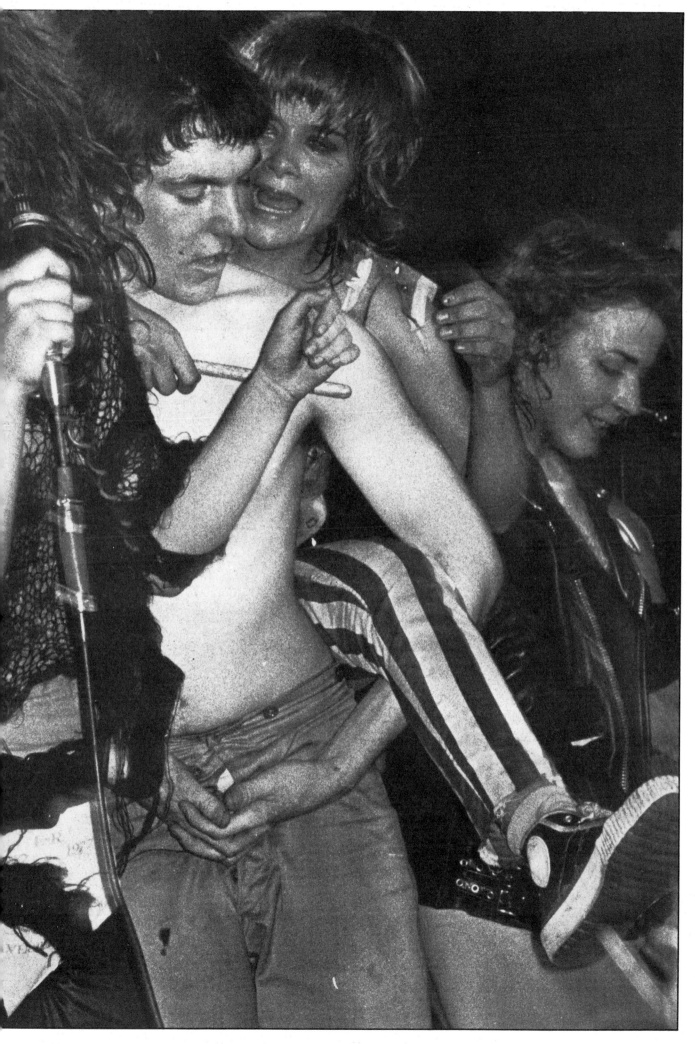

The Adverts

The Adverts
T.V.Smith—Vocals
Gaye Advert—Bass
Howard Pickup—Guitar
Laurie Driver—Drums

One Chord Wonders
I wonder what we'll play for
you tonight,
Something heavy or
something light?
Something to set your soul
alight
I wonder how we'll answer
when you say:
'We don't like you—go away,
Come back when you've
learnt to play'.

I wonder what we'll do when
things go wrong,
When we're half way through
our favourite song,
I look up and the audience
has gone.

If we feel a little bit obscure,
Think 'We're not needed
here—
We must be New Wave, they'll
like us next year'.
(Smith)

Don't stick us down as the
future 'cos we'll change it'.
T. Smith

Bored Teenagers
We're just bored teenagers,
Looking for love, or should I
  say emotional rages,
Bored teenagers,
Looking for hope, or should I
  say emotional rages,
Bored teenagers,
Seeing ourselves as strangers.
(Smith)

'T.V. would probably be
playing this sort of music
anyway. It just happens to
have coincided with, what is
basically, new music and new
outlook for young people'.
Howard Pickup

SUBWAY SECT

Subway Sect
Vic Godard — Vocals
Robert Miller — Guitar
Paul Myers — Bass
Paul Smith — 1st drummer
Mark Laff — 2nd Drummer
(left May 1977)

'I care about being involved in society . . . I'm talkin' about being involved in doing things . . . causes that you can stand up for . . . things like that'. *Vic Godard*

'The reason I don't move is . . . if I moved I wouldn't be able to play the bass, I'd miss all the notes, so I just stand still. If it's an image I'm glad it's original anyway . . .' *Paul Myers*

'The music's based on trying to do anything that doesn't sound quite right — if the chords to a song sound anything like a normal "rock song" then we don't use it'. *Subway Sect*

'I always wanna be a teenager and when I'm old I'm not gonna act as an adult. I mean, when people say "you're childish" at the age of 25. Well, when I'm 25 I'm still gonna do things like . . . er . . . dribble'. *Vic Godard*

Eater
ndy Blade—Vocals
rian Chevette—Guitar
an Woodcock—Bass
ee Generate—Drums
eft May 1977)
hilip Roland—Drums
oined June 1977)

'School kids are able to relate
o us. We're the youngest
and on the scene'. *Eater*

'hey (journalists) always ask
tupid questions like "What
oes Mummy think?" "What
bout safety pins?" you know.
hey ask "What's behind it?"
tupid. There's nothing signifi-
ant or shocking about what
e do. We just play for
urselves, to kids like
urselves. There's nothing
ehind it'. *Ian Woodcock*

think if you want to be a
egend you have to die young
ke James Dean or Gene
incent before you get boring'.
ndy Blade

EATER

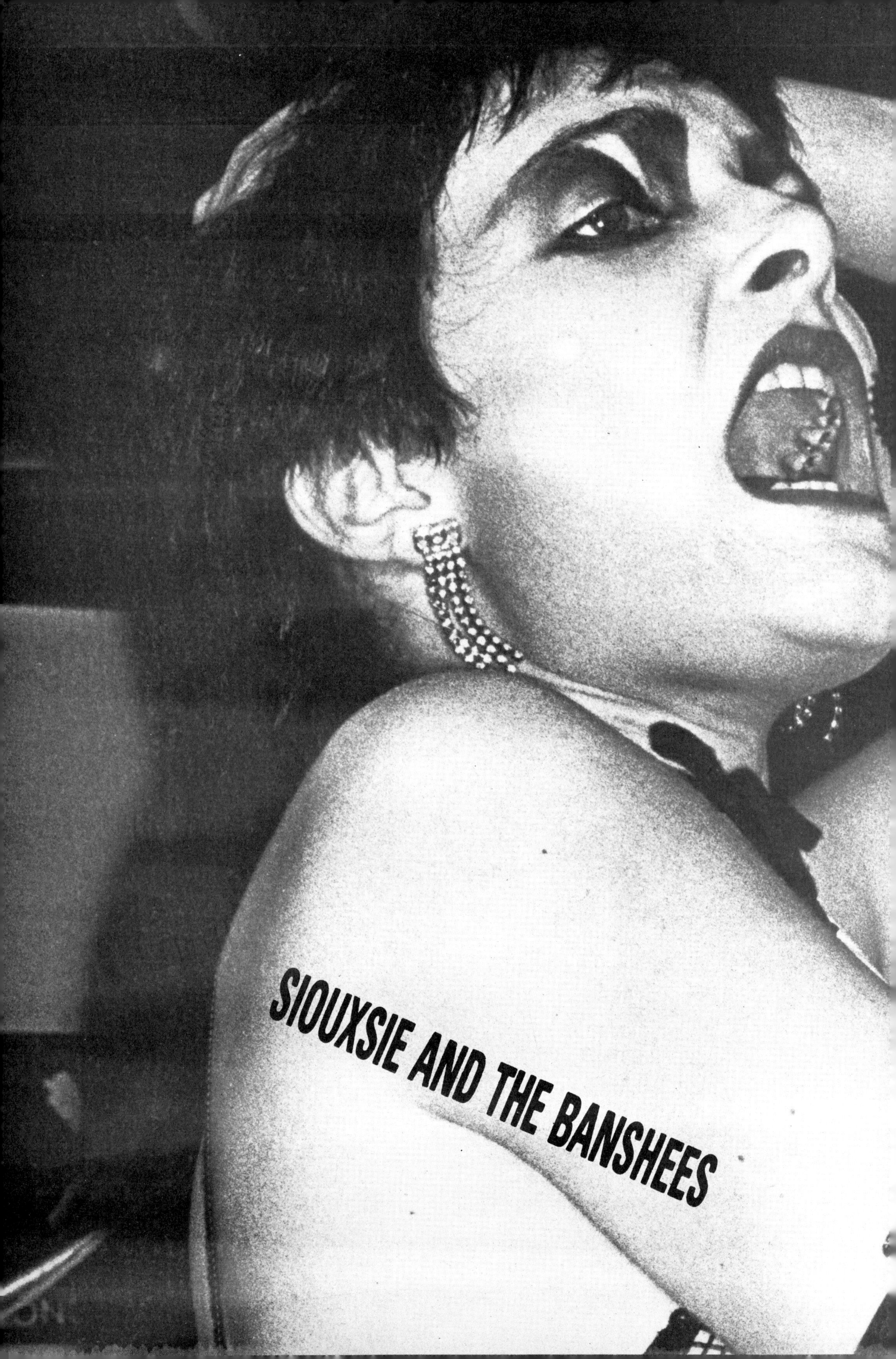

SIOUXSIE AND THE BANSHEES

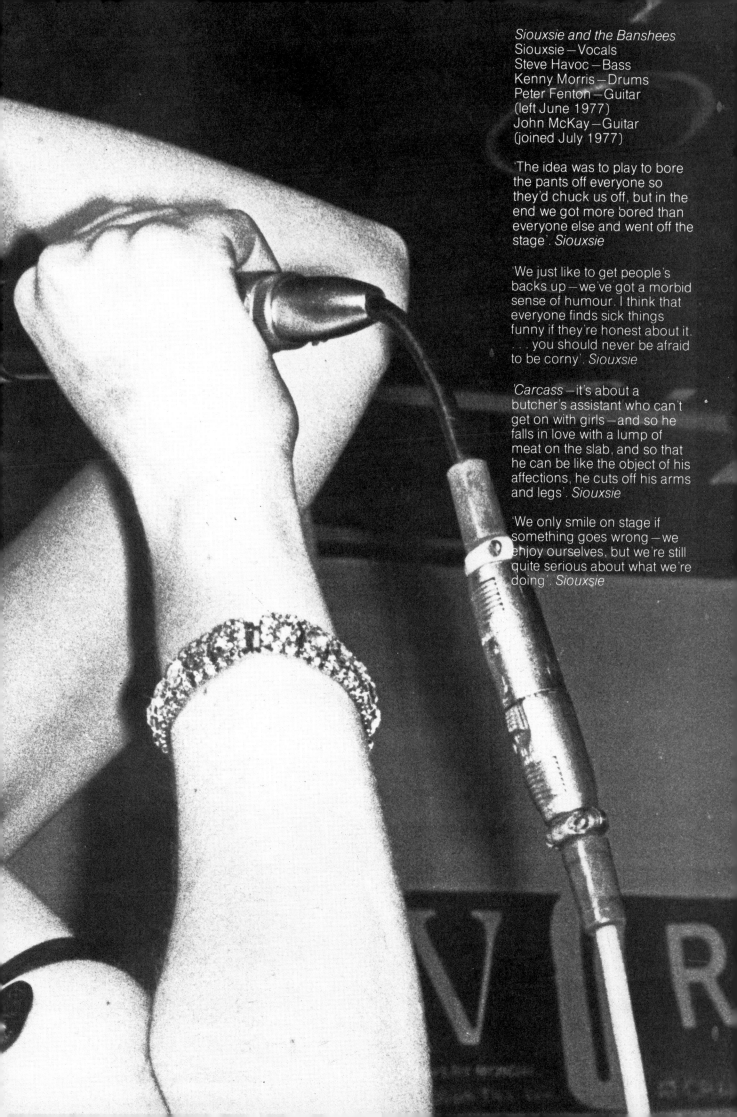

Siouxsie and the Banshees
Siouxsie — Vocals
Steve Havoc — Bass
Kenny Morris — Drums
Peter Fenton — Guitar
(left June 1977)
John McKay — Guitar
(joined July 1977)

'The idea was to play to bore the pants off everyone so they'd chuck us off, but in the end we got more bored than everyone else and went off the stage'. *Siouxsie*

'We just like to get people's backs up — we've got a morbid sense of humour. I think that everyone finds sick things funny if they're honest about it. . . . you should never be afraid to be corny'. *Siouxsie*

'Carcass — it's about a butcher's assistant who can't get on with girls — and so he falls in love with a lump of meat on the slab, and so that he can be like the object of his affections, he cuts off his arms and legs'. *Siouxsie*

'We only smile on stage if something goes wrong — we enjoy ourselves, but we're still quite serious about what we're doing'. *Siouxsie*

'We get to do very few rehearsals — so we don't get much opportunity to write new songs. All I can do is channel all the hatred and frustration into playing drums — work off the aggression on the kit'. *Kenny Morris*

'We're not going to explain ourselves any more, we're just going to do what we want and if no-one understands it that's their problem'. *Siouxsie*

the Vibrators

The Vibrators
Knox—Vocals/guitar
John Ellis—Guitar
Gary Tibbs—Bass
Jon Edwards—Drums

'I'm much older than most
people doing punk. I'm ten
years older I'm the other
generation—like the old lot!
But I like doing the new stuff!
I was playing when the old lot
were in, but I stopped because
I didn't find it very interesting
. . . You get people saying "I've
always been a punk. I've
always fucking done it". I
mean, I've played in fucking
Irish showbands, all that kind
of rubbish. But who cares?'
Knox

'The Vibrators really are the
Blank Generation . . . We're
about not taking it so
seriously'. *Knox*

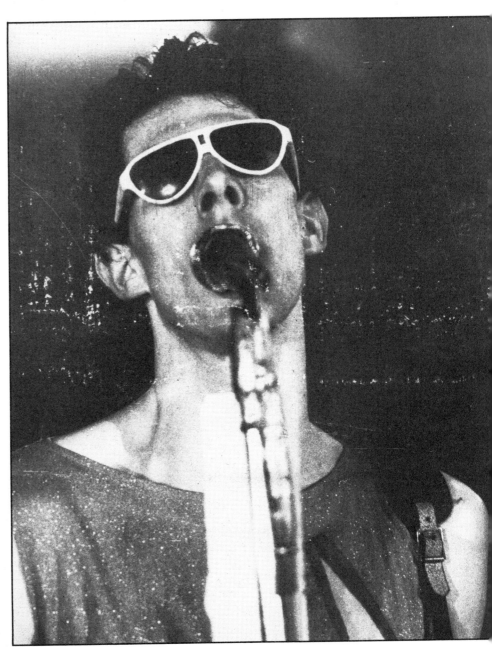

Sham 69
Jimmy Pursey—Vocals
Albie Maskell—Bass
(left September 1977)
Dave Tregannon—Bass
(joined September 1977)
Dave Parsons—Guitar
Mark Cain—Drums

Oxford Street
All foreign feet down Oxford
  Street
Faces from places I've never
  been
All the shops and restaurants
Asking for money I haven't got
It's just a fake
Make no mistake
A rip-off for us
But a Rolls for them.
(©Pursey/Parsons)

'Words are the most important
thing about punk. If I just
wanted to pogo, there's
hundreds of bands I could go
and see—that's just as bad as
Disco. What I'm interested in is
people who tell the truth.
That's what I believe in'. *Jimmy
Pursey*

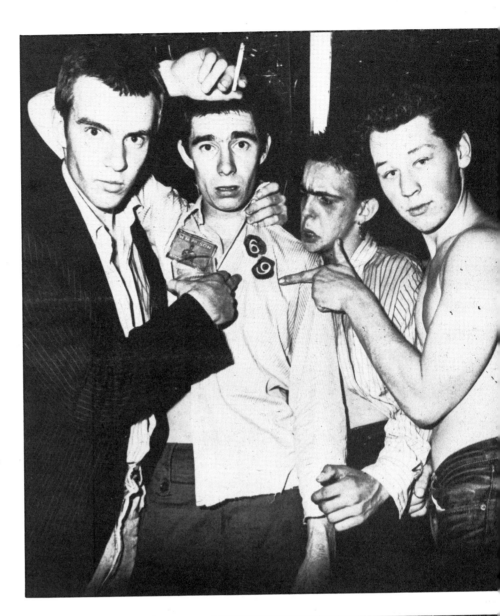

Slaughter and the Dogs
Wayne Barret—Vocals
Mike Rossi—Guitar/vocals
Brian Grantham—Drums
Howard Bates—Bass

'We're just a high energy, Ne
Wave rock'n'roll band . . . wi
style'. *Mike Rossi*

The Boys
Kid Reed — Vocals/bass
Matt Dangerfield — Vocals/
 guitar
Casino Steel — Piano
Jack Black — Drums
Honest John Plain — Guitar

'For most kids there's only one direction you can go — the factory, the office or the dole queue. If you want to get out of that you can either be a footballer or go into rock'. *Kid Reed*

e Cortinas
remy Valentine — Vocals
ck Sheppard — Rhythm guitar
ke Fewins — Lead guitar
an Swann — Bass
exter — Drums

'*e*'re not pretending to be
le queue members. We're
ddle class and we go to
hool. I can't be a punk
hen I'm forty, so I'm learning
play tenor sax. Then I can
off and play at Butlin's
hen I'm past it'. *Jeremy*
lentine

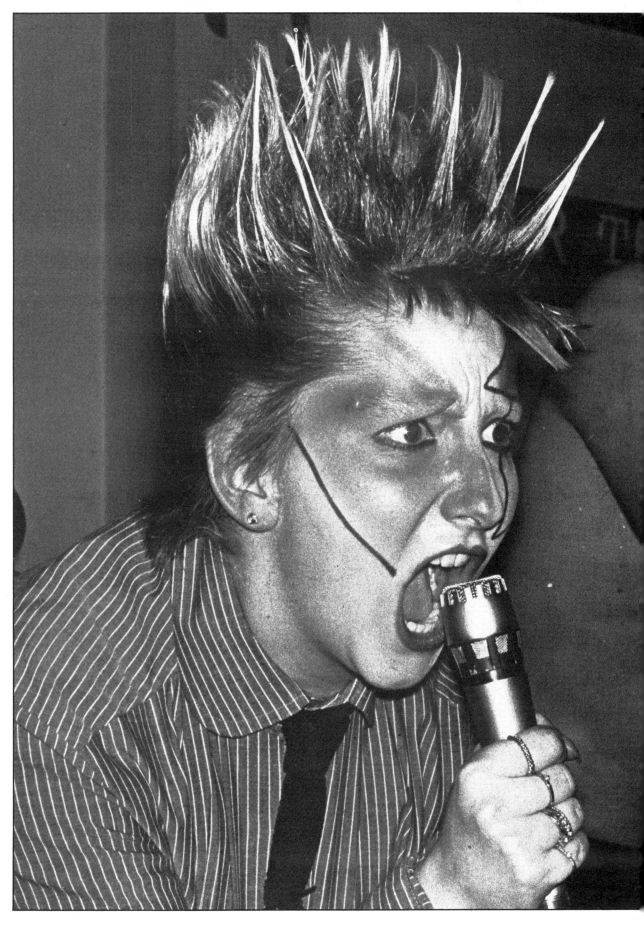

The Ants
Adam Ant—Vocals
Dave Barb—Drums
Johnny Bivouac—Guitar
Winkle and Wankle Watson—
   Bass
Jordan—Manager/vocals

X-Ray Spex
Poly Styrene — Vocals
Laura Logic — Saxophone
Jack Crash — Guitar
Paul Dean — Bass
Richard Tee — Drums
(left June 1977)
B.P. — Drums

'They thought "Oh, you can't
have a saxophone in a punk
band" but then people see it
on stage and they see it work,
then everybody likes it . . . The
songs are not all that political.
What I do is to highlight certain
aspects of my surroundings'.
Poly Styrene

Oh Bondage Up Yours!
Bind me, tie me,
Chain me to the wall
I wanna be a slave
 to you all

Oh bondage up yours
Oh bondage no more
Oh bondage up yours
Oh bondage no more

Chain-store, chain-smoke
I consume you all
Chain-gang, chain-mail
I don't think at all

Thrash me, crash me,
Beat me till I fall
I wanna be a victim
 for you all.
(©*Poly Styrene*)

99

The Drones
M. J. Drone — Vocals
Gus — Guitar
Steve Cundall — Bass
Pete Howells — Drums

Alternative TV
Mark P — Vocals
Tyrone Thomas — Bass
Dennis Burns — Bass
Chris Bennet — Drums

How Much Longer
'How much longer will people
   wear
Nazi armbands and dye their
   hair
Safety pins and spray their
   clothes
Talk about anarchy, fascism
   and boredom
We don't know nothing and
   we don't really care'.
(Mark P.)

999
Nick Cash — Vocals/guitar
Guy Days — Guitar/vocals
Jon Watson — Bass
Pablo Labritan — Drums

The Models
Cliff Fox-Guitar/vocals
Marco Pirroni—Guitar
Mick Allen—Bass
Terry Day—Drums

Penetration
Pauline—Vocals
R. Blamire—Bass
Gary Chaplin—Guitar
Gary Smallman—Drums

The Lurkers
Howard Wall—Vocals
Pete Stride—Guitar
Nigel—Bass
Maniac Esso—Drums

The Ramones
Joey Ramone – Vocals
Johnny Ramone – Guitar
Dee Dee Ramone – Bass
Tommy Ramone – Drums

'When we started it was the big glitter-rock thing….flashy clothes and platforms, so we thought we'd just go on in what we wore in the street. In the beginning we'd play numbers like *Sniffin' Glue*.'
Joey Ramone

Wanna Sniff Some Glue
Now I wanna sniff some glue,
Now I wanna have somethin'
   to do,
All the kids wanna sniff some
   glue,
All the kids want somethin' to
   do.
(The Ramones)

'We never had jobs, rock 'n' roll was the only sort of thing we could do…We don't want to get into a big intellectual thing. We just want to play rock 'n' roll. Just being original is showing intelligence.'
Johnny Ramone

'The thing is we are raw energy. We always are. We always will be. We like energy.'
Tommy Ramone

Television
Tom Verlaine – Vocals/guitar
Richard Lloyd – Guitar/vocals
Fred Smith – Bass/vocals
Billy Ficca – Drums

'I like the energy of so-called Punk music, but I don't like the sound of it.' *Tom Verlaine*

AMERICAN NEW WAVE

Talking Heads
David Byrne — Vocals/guitar
Martina Weymouth — Bass
Jerry Harrison — Keyboards
Chris Franz — Drums

'Working with a group is like
consciously trying to annihilate
the idea of there being an
individual who is a hero.'
Talking Heads

The Heartbreakers
Johnny Thunder —
   Vocals/guitar
Walter Lure — Guitar
Billy Rath — Bass
Jerry Nolan — Drums

'We're just a regular rock 'n'
roll band.' *Johnny Thunder*

'Much as I love New York and
it's my home, England's really
where it's happening now,
musically.' *Walter Lure*

Cherry Vanilla
Cherry Vanilla — Vocals
Louie Lepore — Guitar
Zecca Esquibel — Keyboards

'That's how you tell if the London kids like you, right? If they like you they pogo!'
Cherry Vanilla

Electric Chairs
Wayne County — Vocals
Greg Van Cook — Guitar
Val Haller — Bass
J. J. Johnson — Drums

'I just wanna have a rock 'n' roll band really.' *Wayne County*

'My early sets were more or less a freak show with rock music behind it.'
Wayne County

Patti Smith Band
Patti Smith — Vocals
Lenny Kaye — Guitar
Ivan Kral — Guitar
Richard Sohl — Keyboards
Jay Daugherty — Drums

'I'd much rather be remembered for rock 'n' roll — it's the highest thing happenin'.' *Patti Smith*

'We love the kids in England; they really have more heart and more intuitive understanding of rock 'n' roll than any audience in the world.' *Lenny Kaye*

White Stuff
1st Issue — February 1977
Scotland
'The first issue had a major portion devoted to Patti Smith and the magazine is named after a line in one of her songs…Patti Smith is the single most important artist to emerge this decade…'
Sandy Robertson (24)

Garage Land
1st Issue — December 1976
Newcastle
'My personal faves, Iggy and the Stooges, Clash, Pistols (obviously), Patti Smith, Buzzcocks, Talking Heads, Ramones…and of the "old wave" I like the Doors, and the Velvet Underground.'
Andi (19)

Blondie
Debbie Harry — Vocals
Chris Stein — Guitar
Gary Valentine — Bass
Jimmy Destri — Keyboards
Clement Burke — Drums

'We're a rock 'n' roll band not a punk band and when you take away all the -isms and -osophies that's what it all comes down to — the basic rock and roll elements.'
Jimmy Destri

FASH

'You have to be pretty
eccentric to shock anyone.
You went through the early
seventies and no one turned a
blind eye down the King's
Road. It was only when you
got people wearing
outrageous make-up, clothes
that weren't from Take 6, that's
when you started shocking
people. It just took off from
there . . .' *Nigel Bricknell of
Smuts/Punk clothes shop*

'Malcolm's shop was a great place to go. The clothes were always different. It was new and good and honest. It was anti-fashion and anti-establishment'. *Johnny Rotten*

'It was great then, it was really nice — very rough sort of shop. The clothes went down in history'. *Jordan*

'I opened the shop because I wanted people to make a certain statement if they wore my clothes'. *Malcolm McLaren, Co-owner with Vivienne Westwood of the shop Let it Rock/Too Fast to Live/Sex/Seditionaries*

'I think that many people had got to the end of their tether. They were forced to buy off the peg, mass produced clothes . . . Vivienne created a new market, something extreme. She was artistic enough to have started it and was born out of total boredom with the clothes that the kids had to wear'. *Jordan*

'My clothes are a commitment. You can't walk down the road in them and avoid a confrontation'. *Vivienne Westwood*

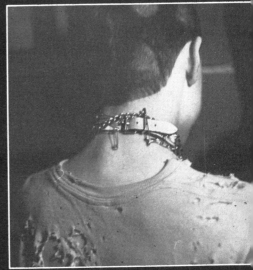

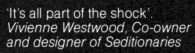

'It's all part of the shock'.
Vivienne Westwood, Co-owner
and designer of Seditionaries

'. . . the safety pin thing has
really a lot to do with John
(Rotten). He started to rip his
clothes and put safety pins in
and they really latched onto
that through the press . . .'
Jordan

'A punk wears his clothes.
He's making an outward sign
that he's rebelling'.

'As with any rock'n'roll fashio
thing, at the moment it all ties
up, the music, fashion,
everything, make-up, the
whole thing'. *Nigel Bricknell*
Smuts

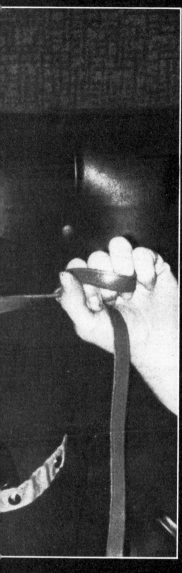

'It's the first time since the mods and rockers that kids are wearing clothes that evolved from their own life-style'. *Vivienne Westwood*

'I had a tiepin on the other day, just a paper clip and a bloke came up and said "Ah, good tiepin"... I said "It's only a paperclip John, d'ya want it?"... He said "Should be in gold, what!" What's he talking about? He's treating my life as a game, it's this week's trend, it's this week's fad, Punk Rock, right?' *Danny Baker*

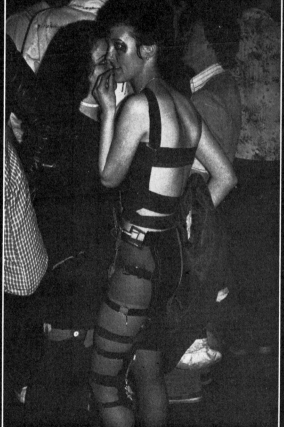

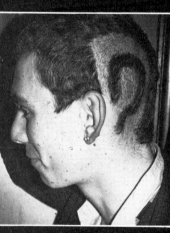

THE ROXY CLUB

'Get along and see all the punk rock you can 'cos that's the only way somebody's going to be interested in opening some sort of club for these bands . . . I wanna go out and hear the sounds I like every night.' *Mark P.*

'Just through chance and talking to Chelsea's Gene October, he put me in contact with a guy who had a club which wasn't doing very well and we zoomed in straight away and hired it one night in December . . . People did turn up and it was sufficient to pay the rent and it was a bit of fun and the band (Generation X) did eventually play . . . So we decided to do it again the following week—at the time the Heartbreakers were over from America, they were at a loose end and couldn't get too much work so we booked them in straight away . . . I ran the club permanently from January—it became 24 hours a day—the Clash (Jan 1st) was the official first night of the new period . . . *Andy Czezowski—Manager of Roxy Club*

'We never advertised, never wanted to, we purely worked on handouts'. *Andy Czezowski*

'People did literally ring up the club and say: "I've got this new punk band, and we want to play — we've never played before, but we've been rehearsing for a night and we feel we ought to play!" I used to book them, because I felt, well, that's the spirit of things, that these kids could simply pick up a guitar because they wanted to, prance around and show off on stage, and I was just providing them with an outlet for it'. *Andy Czezowski*

'I was getting more asking me for reggae than punk . . . At first, I wasn't sure whether to play it or not but then again, there wasn't enough material out. Like they say, I'm D.J'ing at the Roxy . . . but there's no D.J'ing to do!' *Don Letts*

'We just let the people have fun. If they stomped on a few plastic glasses, who cares? They're only 1p each. They jumped onto the ceiling and stood on the seats, and jumped on the glasses to smash up the plastic and there was graffiti everywhere, and in that sense it was wild because you'd not be able to do that anywhere else'. *Andy Czezowski*

'The whole pogo dancing business was frowned upon because it didn't look like normal dancing, therefore it looked a bit more like trouble, and trouble normally was caused by the fact that people didn't understand the fact that they were pogoing, y'know, jumping up and down . . .'
Andy Czezowski

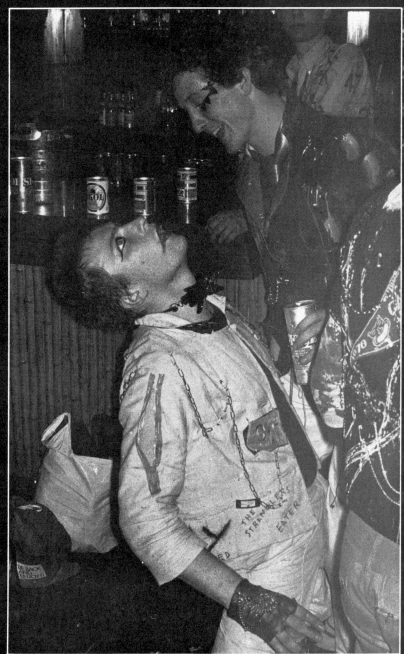

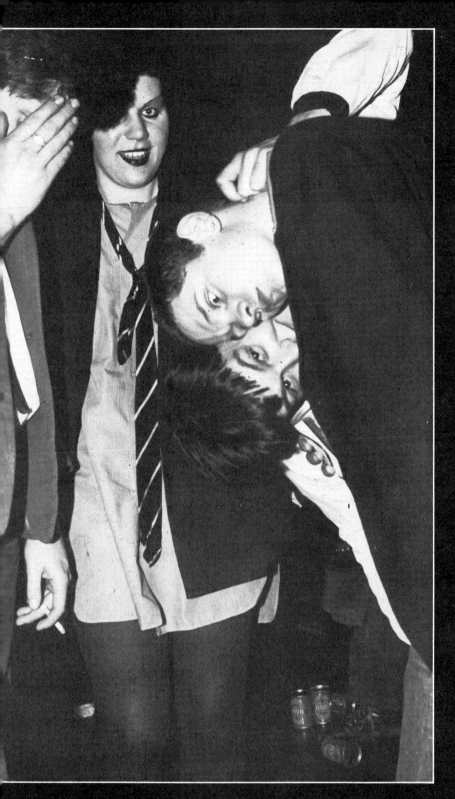

'That's why I did the album "Live at the Roxy" because I saw those people coming in — the kids — and I could see myself as one of them queuing up outside, paying like £1 to get into the club, and they thoroughly enjoyed themselves'. *Andy Czezowski*

'The thing sort of developed, it was like a catalyst really. Also people met, bands met, they progressed, they exchanged ideas, formed ideas . . . Band management I think will always be similar . . . looking after four kids and changing their nappies, giving them drinks, and getting them on stage on time'. *Andy Czezowski*

'It was up and down—it was going to close and then it wasn't. It was genuine, in no way calculated by us to make it. I think all the spirit went . . . We wanted to make the Roxy a breeding ground for new groups. . . . It came at the right time—but now it's time to move on . . . *Andy Czezowski*

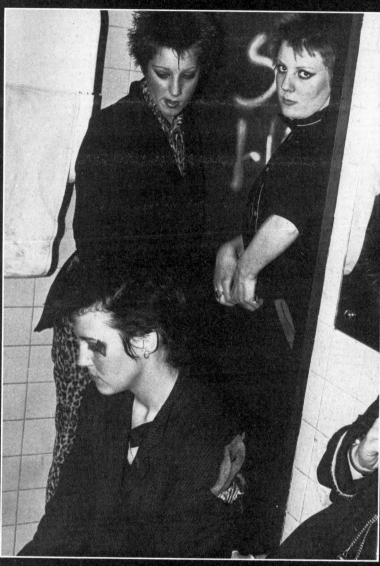

·SORRY· THE GROUP CANCELLED AT THE LAST MINUTE . SO WERE CLOSED TONIGHT

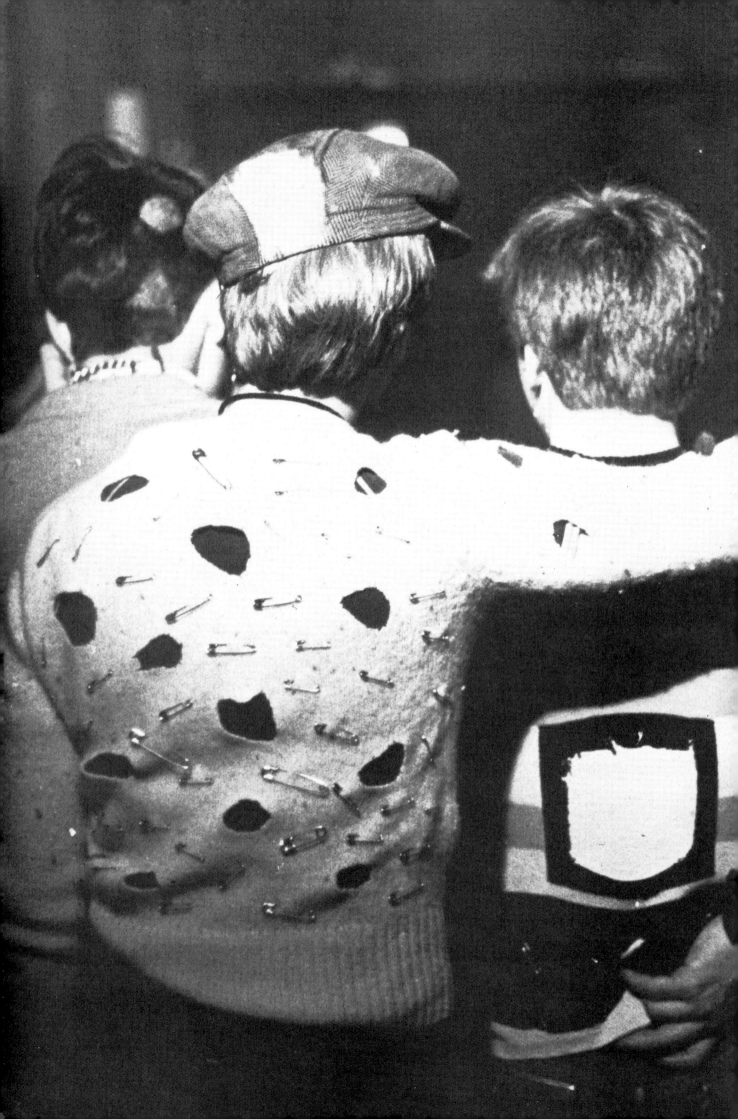

'It's for the love of rock 'n' roll that you spend all those nights practising.' *Tony James*

'We'll go on until we feel that there's no point in our format.' *Hugh Cornwell*

'We'll only finish the day it gets boring.' *Johnny Rotten*

CREDITS
All the fanzines, ZigZag, Punk
Magazine, New Musical
Express, Record Mirror,
Sounds, The Observer, the
Sunday Times, the Herald
Tribune, & Martin Baker for
allowing me to use interview
material from his film Raw
Energy.

ACKNOWLEDGEMENTS
Special thanks to the following
fanzine writers: Mark & Danny
of Sniffin' Glue, Tony of
Ripped & Torn, Alan of Live
Wire, Adrian of 48 Thrills, Rick
of Skum, Andi of Garage
Land, Pete & Piers of Shews,
Charlie of Chainsaw, Jon of
London's Outrage, John
Jacques of Stranded, Max of
Tomorrow The World, Steve of
Shy Talk, Dave of Rotten to the
Core, Ade & Nag of New
Wave, Ronnie of Gun Rubber,
Lee & Roy of Viva La
Resistance, Jon of Negative
Reaction, Craig of Trash,
Martin & Mick of Ghast Up,
Glen and Jon of Flicks, Tim of
Cliche, Arcane of These
Things, Sandy of White Stuff,
Tony of Sideburns/Strangled,
Jonh of London's Burning,
Martin of New Pose, Sarah
and Crystal of More On.

I would like to thank all those
who wrote in but were unable
to be included for lack of
space.

I would like to thank for their
help, support & time: Pete &
Bruce at Town Records, Jeff &
Steve of Rough Trade, Sophie
R., Sue L., Kim, Suzanna,
Vivienne, Danny, Erica, Mark
P., Brian, Jane A., Jonh I.,
Nils, Jordan, Simon, Adam,
Tony J., Nick J., Michael L.,
Walt D., Ron W., Kris, Nigel B.,
Paulo, Don L., John K., John
W., Falcon, Harry F., Derek J.,
Jon, Andy C., Steve, Pete,
Piers, Sheila, Ken & all the
photographers who
contributed.

Thanks to Erica, Mac and
Martin W. for initiation, Angela
& Christina for moral support
& Derek for understanding

PICTURE CREDITS
Jane Ashley 108/9; Jo-anne
Atkinson 72, 73tl,tr,cl;
Richard Braine 6, 7, 10/11,
33b, 76b; CBS 35b; Kevin
Cummins 75t, 85l, 96b, 100t,
101b, 102b; Walt Davidson
18/19, 58, 59t, 78t,c,b, 85r,
89, 123b; Erica Echenberg
27, 35t, 38, 39t, 42/3, 44tl,
45t, 46t, 56, 60, 61t, 74, 88,
96t, 100bl, 115 inset; Jill
Furmanovsky 67t; Glitterbest
20 inset; Bob Gruen 9, 103b;
Jonh Ingham 39b, 46bl, 46/7,
87; J. R. 22bl, 124/5; Peter
Kodick 21 insets, 28b, 45b,
46bl, 64/5, 104b; Dennis
Morris/Virgin 8, 29, 30b,
31bl,br; Norma Morrisey 110,
111; Harry Murlowski 26/7,
28t, 59b, 61b, 97l, 121tr;
NEMS 97r; Paulo Nozolino
115; Pete of Shews 44tr,
102/3; Polydor 56/57; Derek
Ridgers 1, 4, 5, 10, 12, 26br,
32, 33t, 40, 41, 54, 55, 62b,
63, 65c inset, 68, 69,
73cr,bl,br, 76, 77tl,tr, 78/9,
80/81, 84, 90/91, 93, 98,
100br, 101tl, 105b, 107, 116,
117, 120, 122tl,r, 123r; Mick
Rock 22t, 106; Sheila Rock
44b, 52b, 65t. inset, 67b, 77b,
110tl, 114; Sire 102tl; Step
Forward 65 b.inset; Ray
Stevenson 20/21, 22br, 23,
26bl, 53t, 66/7b, 70/71, 82/3,
92t, 95, 105; Track Records
104/5; United Artists 49, 50,
51, 52t, 53b; Virgin Records
2/3, 8, 29, 30/31, 99; Annette
Wetherman 14/15, 34, 36,
36/7, 37, 62tl,tr, 66/7t, 75b,
86, 89, 92b, 94, 112/3, 112,
113, 120tl, 120/1, 121b,
122b, 123l, 124, 125, 126/7.